SOCIAL MEDIA MARKETING TIPS 2019

Build Your Brand And Become An Expert In Digital Networking & Personal Branding, Create Your Business With Facebook, Instagram, Youtube And Twitter Using Effective Mastery Influencer Strategies

Jason Miller, Robert McDonald

ISBN: 9781079799019

Printed in USA

Table of Contents

4

Chapter One

SOCIAL MEDIA MARKETING TIPS

Social media marketing is a completely new, but vital part of online marketing that has taken off in the last few years. A brief definition of it is the process of increasing traffic to your site or gaining attention online though social media sites.

The first step in a profitable social media marketing campaign is locating the audience. Millions of people use the Internet to find their ideal product or service, but it is impossible to get your product or service to the people if you don't know who they are. With the Internet providing such a massive user-base, it is incredibly difficult to pull specific people out of the crowd. Social media makes it much easier through the use of relevant images, videos, or written content that leads people to your website.

If you really want to run a successful Internet marketing campaign, it will pay you to learn a few social media marketing tips, and apply them to your efforts. Simple tips can create lasting results, and sometimes propel a company to instant success. Remember though, that instant success is the exception, not the rule, and always follow the most important tip of all: Be Patient.

One of the most common social media marketing tips is to actively participate. Post on related message forums, publish blogs, and submit article to similarly article directories. Get your company and its products in front of many people as possible in a way that is helpful and informative. Show your potential customers why your company is the one that they should be telling their friends about. Many lists of social media marketing tips are clear about another point, as well - Be Consistent. Your identity should not differ a great deal from one social media site to another. Always maintain a professional appearance, and provide open friendly communication. Build trust in your company and products by supporting them in the same clear manner, regardless of where you may be approached. Another important item, according to popular social media marketing tips, is to broaden your horizons. It is a good idea to have a particular target audience, but do not underestimate the power of social networks to cross those target boundaries. Appeal to a wide range of Internet communities and networks in addition to your focused strategies.

Encourage people to spread the word. Your best sales representatives don't work for you at all, but are the result of your online marketing strategies. Ordinary people who are interested in your products and services will happily tell their friends, refer your site to the social bookmarking sites like Digg, and paste your URL in email and on blogs. Capitalize on this by offering complete customer support and exceptional service.

Word of mouth is a powerful tool, and many social media marketing tips point out that your best promotion comes from allowing others to sell you to their associates. To do this, you have to provide quality content, informative information, and products that appeal to people enough that they want to talk about them to their friends. Social networking is all about communication and sharing

Everybody who knows anything about internet marketing will tell you that social media marketing is one of the best tools to use if you want to succeed in marketing your business on the World Wide Web. This involves implementing several strategies to make one's marketing tools more easily available to the targeted audience.

The first step in a profitable social media marketing campaign is locating the audience. Millions of people use the Internet to find their ideal product or service, but it is impossible to get your product or service to the people if you don't know who they are. With the Internet providing such a massive user-base, it is incredibly difficult to pull specific people out of the crowd. Social media makes it much easier through the use of relevant images, videos, or written content that leads people to your website.

Produce Fresh Content Regularly.

If you are running a website of your own, write fresh content on a daily basis if possible. There may be a larger gap between posts, but it is not advised to stretch beyond the length of a few days. The readers will quickly go to one of your competitor's if it's providing fresh content and your information becomes stale. Current events and news are great sources, but they aren't likely to draw the widest possible range of potential.

Make Your Branding Strong.

Make sure that your branding is strong and that you encourage your followers to identify with it, this will encourage them to follow your business throughout all of its ups and downs. Think very carefully about what you post online, one mistake could come back to haunt you many months down the line and in extreme cases could ruin your brand completely. A strong brand is a powerful tool that can create excellent public awareness if used correctly. High-quality content that carries your name will establish respect from the community and drive traffic for years to come.

Encourage Customer Interaction

Create a spot on your website that is entirely dedicated to customer-interactions. This area will benefit the company by providing an open forum for discussion, concerns, and personal stories. Though it is designed for the readers, it is still a great idea to keep an eye on what is being discussed and to use this information for making improvements. Encourage your subscribers to share their own media and content; circulating different videos, music, or images that they enjoy. Use the most popular media as a template for your own productions and publish content that Centre's around similar ideas.

Make Use of Social Bookmarking.

Use social media bookmarks to create a link between your own webpages and useful content that is spread elsewhere across the web. Bandwidth limitations may make it difficult to host various forms of media, but social media bookmarks provide an easy solution. Rather than hosting the original file, your website includes a favicon or link that leads to the social media domain and the particular posting. Bookmarks are also a great way to share content that is impossible to obtain without infringing various copyright laws.

The complex practices behind social media marketing were briefly touched on in this article, but there is so much more to learn about this massive subject. Take some time to read through the tips a second time and begin mapping out your social media campaign. These basics are a great place to start, but bear in mind that there are still several in-depth concepts to be mastered.

Are you in charge of getting your company's social media marketing up and running? Using social media to grow your business generate leads and build a brand may seem like a huge task, and in some ways it is. But there are steps you can follow to improve your chances of success, which will help you take advantage of everything social media has to offer.

Whether you're just getting started or have been active on sites like Facebook and Twitter, but haven't had much success, follow these 21 social media marketing tips to propel you to the next level:

1. Create a Social Media Plan for Each Social Media Channel

If you fail to plan, you plan to fail. So many businesses make the mistake of blindly jumping into social media marketing without a strategy or plan.

If you can't answer questions like "why are you on social media?" or "what social media platform features your target audience?" then it's time to hit the reset button. Start putting together a plan in writing that you and your team can refer to when you need it. Your social media plan should consist of mini-plans for each social media channel you expect to be active on. You'll have a plan for your Twitter, Facebook and so forth.

If you're just getting started, keeps your number of active social networking sites to three or less. For most businesses, particularly small businesses, trying to tackle five different social media accounts often results in doing a mediocre job with little to no results.

Not sure where to start? Check out our free guide, 7 Steps to Create a Winning Social Media Marketing Strategy.

2. Post Consistently

Sending out one Tweet per day just isn't going to cut it. Certain platforms like Instagram and Snapchat don't necessarily move as fast as Twitter or Facebook. This means you don't have to publish as often. But you should still develop a routine posting schedule and be consistent.

These ties back in with your social media marketing plan. You should outline:

• How often you plan to publish on each social media channel

• What type of content you plan to publish

• Social media outreach publishing schedule (reaching out to influencers via social media)

Remember your followers are likely following hundreds or even thousands of other people. If you're not publishing new content as often as the other accounts out there, it's easy to get lost and forgotten.

3. Be Picky About What You Share

When it comes to figuring out what to share on social media, quality beats quantity. You want to publish content consistently, but it also has to be valuable. Quality content is:

- Relevant to your audience

- Helpful

- Entertaining

One trend becoming popular that you should be cautious of is relying on tools that "suggest" content to share to your audience. Sometimes the suggestions are decent, but in most cases, you'll end up with a lot of suggested content that isn't very relevant or high quality.

These tools typically run based on keywords and data feeds. If you didn't take the time to check the suggestions and just blindly added the posts, you'd be sharing content that's not really helpful to your audience. Strive to share the best content, not just what's immediately available.

One way to have a steady supply of fresh content is to create a list of sites in your industry or niche that are known to publish high quality content. Add them to an RSS reader like Feedly. Then you'll have a dashboard full of the latest posts from sites you trust and know have relevant content that you can confidently share with your followers.

You can even integrate Feedly within the Sprout Social dashboard

4. Use a Social Media Management Tool

If you're using the native publishing platforms for Facebook, Twitter and LinkedIn, you're wasting time and being less productive. Social media management tools like Sprout Social make it a lot easier to:

• Publish content across multiple platforms

• Schedule posts in advance

• Collaborate with your team

• See all of your social media feeds from a single dashboard instead of logging into five different sites

• Track and measure your results

There are plenty of other benefits to using a social media dashboard, but those instances alone are more than enough to make the move. The casual user may be able to stick with managing their social media from their phones, but as a business, you need to use a tool that will allow you to be more efficient and strategic.

5. Post More Images

The results are in and photos have shown to be the most popular type of social media content for engagement. They get the most shares on Facebook. And the most Retweets on Twitter.

The most evident example of the power of images for social media is sites like Instagram and Pinterest, which are primarily driven by images. In fact, Instagram has the most engagement of any social media channel. It's not a coincidence that both Instagram and Pinterest were able to gain a lot of traction and see more success than other failed social networks.

Adding images to your social media posts has never been easier. Tools like Canva and Landscape allow you to create perfectly-sized images that are fit for all major social media channels. And you can also do things like use images for upcoming events, make company photos and craft other image tasks for posts to get more visual with your content.

Don't forget to add Twitter Cards to your website so any blog posts you Tweet will have a featured image

6. A/B Test

This is a tip that a lot of social media marketing professionals take advantage of, but not many small businesses on social media are even aware of. A/B testing or split testing, involves using multiple headlines for the same piece of content to see which generates a better response. Marketers use A/B testing a lot for landing pages and sales pages, but you can also incorporate split testing into your social media posts. Instead of publishing a Tweet or Facebook post once and then forgetting about it, schedule the link to be shared multiple times and change the headline out with each post.

A/B testing is important because people will react differently to a post depending on the copy. In our post, Call to Action Phrases That Will Convert, we went over some of the psychology of words and how we interpret them. The reason why a piece of content is lacking success on social media could be due to low quality content or that your headline in the Tweet, Pin or Facebook post didn't capture your followers' attention.

Use Sprout Social's post planning feature to schedule your posts to be shared throughout the week and test different headlines. Then see which one has the best engagement.

7. Measure & Analyze

To go along with the previous social media marketing tip, you need to measure your efforts and analyze the results. Over 40% of businesses don't track their social media ROI at all, so they have no idea whether or not anything they're doing is working. If you don't want to fall under that umbrella, start tracking your social media activity right now.

Some of the metrics that you want to look for include:

• Reach and engagement for Facebook

• Impressions, visits and mentions on Twitter

- Impressions, clicks and interactions on LinkedIn

- Impressions and engagement on Pinterest

- Likes, comments and mentions on Instagram

You should track these metrics on a weekly, monthly and quarterly basis so you know when and if you need to make changes to your social media strategy.

8. Don't Be Afraid to Pay-to-Play

Facebook and other social media networks continue to significantly reduce the amount of organic visibility on your posts, which has more businesses resorting to paid social media advertising to get their message out there. Whether it's boosting a post or promoting a Tweet, social media advertising is a lot more common as these platforms start to grow. If you want to accelerate your social media marketing efforts and have a budget for it, exploring paid advertising might be worth a try. The costs are generally lower than other platforms like Google AdWords or even media buying, which makes social media advertising appealing for small businesses and startups.

On top of that, you have nice targeting options like a user's interests and detailed demographics. If you're new to paid social media advertising, here's a good starter kit that'll show you some of the basics.

9. Join in on Communities

Within large social networks, smaller communities form. Whether it's Facebook Groups, Twitter Chats or LinkedIn Groups, there are plenty of opportunities for you connect with like-minded people and companies within your niche. Participating in these communities will help you establish yourself or your company as an authority. Use communities as an opportunity to share your knowledge and interact with influencers. As you start to connect with these influencers, they'll be more likely to share your content with their followers on social media and maybe even on their own websites.

Look for communities related to your industry on the social media channels you're active on, then start joining and actively participating. Try starting with Facebook groups or Twitter Chats because they tend to be the most active. But this can vary.

10. Build a Community

What if there aren't any existing communities for your industry, or none that are active? Then it's the perfect time for you to be proactive and create one.

Assuming that your industry has a decent amount of people active on a social media channel, start reaching out to let interested people know you're starting a Facebook group, Twitter Chat or LinkedIn Group and you'd like to invite interested users to join.

Some ideas for groups you could start are:

• A local small business group for your city.

• Groups of people within your industry.

• Groups with other companies related to your industry. For example, real estate agents, mortgage brokers and construction companies.

A lot of the time, there is a desire for groups, but either nobody thought of the idea or they just didn't take the effort to put it together. You can be a trailblazer and lead the group.

11. Interact

This social media marketing tip can be a game changer. Don't be the company that only shares links all day. The purpose of social media is to be social and engage with other users. That means interacting on a regular basis. Take a look at some of your past social media posts. How many of them include @mentions of other people? How many of your interactions are replies to other posts? If you're like a lot of companies, then the answer is probably not many. Instead, your social media stream is probably filled with broadcast posts (a headline/message with a link to an article or just text).

You've repeatedly seen the advice of engaging with your audience. But what exactly does that mean?

Replying to other peoples' posts even if it doesn't @mention you

• Retweeting

• Liking posts

• Adding people to Twitter lists

• @mentions

Essentially you want to switch from one-way social media posts to two-way posts. The difference is two-way posts encourage conversation and communication. On the other hand, one-way posts leave little to no room for anyone to reply back with anything other than "good post" or another generic response.

If you're sharing a link, ask for feedback and opinions or tag someone so they'll reply. Think of your social media posts as a part of a conversation.

12. Watch Your Competitors

Is one of your competitors absolutely killing it on social media? Does it seem like all of their Tweets get dozens of Retweets and their Instagram posts have hundreds of likes, while yours are completely abandoned? When this happens, you should start to analyze what they're doing that you aren't.

Look at:

• The content they post

• Who they follow

• Who's following them

• How often they post

• What time of the day they post

• What kind of headlines they use in their posts

• Their most popular posts

This will give you an idea of what's working for your competitors and why they might be seeing more social media success. Once you start to get a feel for your competitor's strategies, you'll want to incorporate some of what they do into your own plan. At the same time, you don't want to completely copy a competitor. For instance, if you notice a competitor posts a lot of images, then start creating more images of your own. Try posting at similar times of the day, or more frequently based on their activity.

However, this isn't an excuse to mimic your competitors to the bone. Your customers will want you to be unique and you should show that by adopting some things from competitors and looking for other ways to improve those strategies.

13. Give People a Reason to Follow You

Why should people follow your company? This is the question you need to ask yourself.

Think of it from the perspective of a consumer. They have thousands of choices of people to follow, so you have to stand out somehow.

Create a type of value proposition specifically for your social media channels. For example:

• You share behind the scenes content on Instagram

• You share discount codes exclusively with your Twitter followers

- You curate the best content in your industry on LinkedIn
- You offer real-time customer service and support on Twitter
- You host live webinars on Periscope

The value has to be exclusive to the social media channel. If you regularly share the same discount codes through email or on your website that you post on Twitter, there's no added value there. Make coupons exclusively for social media. Or have content that's only on Snapchat or on live streams with Periscope so there's a sense of urgency.

14. Build Strategic Alliances or Partnerships

The toughest part of building a social media presence is getting those first initial followers. Let's face it, people are a lot less likely to follow a company with only 13 followers and no engagement than the company with 40,000 followers and hundreds of replies and likes on each post.

But how do you get people to notice you when you don't have brand recognition and people don't know your company at all? You partner up with an established company or influencer that already has an active following. Several companies have seen huge success with this technique on Instagram to go from zero followers to thousands within a matter of days or weeks.

This strategy builds off the "Know, Like, Trust" philosophy. The company you're approaching has an audience of loyal followers that know, like and trust them. Getting a shout out will let their followers know they recommend you. This helps their customers know you're a brand to recognize and trust as well. 14. Build Strategic Alliances or Partnerships

The toughest part of building a social media presence is getting those first initial followers. Let's face it, people are a lot less likely to follow a company with only 13 followers and no engagement than the company with 40,000 followers and hundreds of replies and likes on each post.

But how do you get people to notice you when you don't have brand recognition and people don't know your company at all? You partner up with an established company or influencer that already has an active following. Several companies have seen huge success with this technique on Instagram to go from zero followers to thousands within a matter of days or weeks.

This strategy builds off the "Know, Like, Trust" philosophy. The company you're approaching has an audience of loyal followers that know, like and trust them. Getting a shout out will let their followers know they recommend you. This helps their customers know you're a brand to recognize and trust as well.

There are a couple different ways you can get started with this technique. The easiest way to achieve this is through a paid shout out. There are several sites that connect pages with a large following to companies looking to get a shout out to their audience. However, you must be careful and do your research before using one of these services and you should never buy fake followers. There are a couple different ways you can get started with this technique. The easiest way to achieve this is through a paid shout out. There are several sites that connect pages with a large following to companies looking to get a shout out to their audience. However, you must be careful and do your research before using one of these services and you should never buy fake followers. Another way to get trusted brands to promote your company is by building relationships with influencers first and let the opportunity develop organically.

It could start with an email to a high-level brand saying you like their company and the content they create. Then you should share their content and keep in touch. When the opportunity presents itself, develop some type of content or cross-promotional event like a giveaway that'll allow you to reach their audience while also giving them some value as well.

15. Use Keywords in Your Posts

Don't underestimate the power and effectiveness of social search. Sites like Facebook, Twitter, Pinterest and other social networks have search features that operate just like search engines.

When people search for a specific keyword or phrase like #SMM, the site's bots crawl through all of the content on the site including your posts and profile to display the most relevant information. Including keywords and phrases in your social media posts and profile makes your company more searchable.

Social media optimization is becoming more advanced and accurate because these sites and apps have a lot of content needing to be categorized. Get into the habit of using common hashtags, even on Facebook, and relevant keywords within your social media posts so that you have a better chance of being found by people searching for topics related to your industry.

16. Capitalize on Hashtags

Hashtags are easily one of the best ways to organically expand your reach on social media. As we mentioned earlier, organic reach has dropped dramatically on Facebook and Twitter over the years, and Instagram is likely next in line. In order to expand your reach and get more impressions for your posts and Tweets, start incorporating hashtags.

Inserting random hashtags isn't going to be as effective as taking a strategic approach. Research popular hashtags in your industry, as well as more generic and widely used ones. These are the hashtags people are actively searching for on Twitter and Instagram. Adding them to your Tweets and Instagram posts will give your content a better chance of showing up in the search results.

Monitor your hashtag analytics to track which hashtags are generating the most engagement.

17. Explore New Networks

Who says brands have to be restricted to Facebook, Twitter and Instagram? While those three networks will give you the widest reach, it doesn't mean you should neglect smaller or niche networks.

For instance, Medium is a popular network for publishing long form content. It's perfect for gaining thought leadership and sharing your industry expertise. It's not as popular as Facebook or Twitter, but there's a large enough audience to make it worth exploring.

You should also keep your eyes on emerging social networks. Snapchat has been around for years, but it didn't start to take off for marketers until recently. Being able to spot social media platforms like Snapchat early on will give you a leg up on the competition once they become more mainstream.

18. Don't Be Afraid to Sell

Nearly any list of social media marketing tips you find online will warn you about being too promotional. It's true that constantly shoving marketing messages in your audience's face isn't an effective strategy. However, you can also be too conservative with your posts well. Occasionally tweeting a link to your products or promoting something that will earn your company money isn't a bad thing.

The reason promotional posts are often discouraged is because some companies go overboard to the point of becoming spammy.

Keep the majority of your social media content non-promotional. If you send 10 Tweets in a day, at least six or seven should be completely non-promotional. That creates a healthy balance that won't turn most of your followers away.

19. Target Your Social Media Posts

Your followers are not all alike. Even though your business may attract a certain demographic, your audience consists of individuals who may like your brand for different reasons.

For example, consider Microsoft. Microsoft's customers and social media followers can range from gamers to small business owners. These two audiences aren't going to be attracted to the same content.

In order to satisfy these different segments, Microsoft has to share content specifically for each demographic.

Let's say you want to share a post on LinkedIn targeting the finance industry. Your followers who are in IT or the health industry might not find it relevant. Instead of filling their stream with irrelevant content, you can choose to only show that post to people within your network in the finance industry.

20. Use Contests for Audience Growth Spurts

Your number of followers shouldn't be a primary KPI because it doesn't tell the full story of how well you're doing. Having 1,000 engaged followers is better than having 5,000 bots follow you. With that being said, social proof is real. When you're looking for a new restaurant to try for dinner, are you more likely to go to the place with 100 five start reviews or the one with a handful of four star reviews? The same thing applies with social media.

When users see that an account has a large following, they view them as more authoritative and trustworthy. The thought behind this is if you've gotten 10,000 people to follow you, then you must know what you're talking about.

A good way to gather some initial followers when you're starting from scratch is to hold a social media contest. Twitter and Instagram contests encourage users engage with you and promote your brand. There are different types of contests you can host, but the important thing to keep in mind is to make them brand specific.

Giving away generic gifts like an Amazon gift card will attract a lot of freebie seekers with no long term value. Instead, give away prizes that are related to your brand. Here are some more tips for hosting a successful Instagram contest.

21. Get Your Entire Team Involved

Most of the social media marketing tips we've shared so far are executed by the person or team in charge of your marketing. But social media doesn't have to fall solely on the marketing team's shoulders. If your company has employees or multiple departments, encourage them to help your social media marketing efforts. Whether it's contributing content to the blog, following the company's social profiles or other steps, the more involved your team is the better.

A great tool to help employees get involved with your company's social media marketing strategy is Bambu. This tool is an employee advocacy platform that makes it easy for team members to share curated content across their social media platforms.

Here's an example of how you can use Bambu to improve your social media strategy.

When your company publishes a new blog post that you want to promote, you can add it to your team's curated list where employees can share it on their own Facebook, Twitter or LinkedIn profile.

Chapter Two

SOCIAL MEDIA IMPORTANCE 2019

As of the end of 2018, there were 3.196 BILLION social media users! That's nearly half of the planet! With that volume of users, businesses can no longer ignore the necessity and benefits of social media marketing. These numbers continue to grow exponentially each year and with the increase in users, the increase in sales via social media content marketing follows suit.

Social media has changed the way we live our lives. From the way we get our news to the way we interact with our loved ones. Social media is everywhere. It's unavoidable, it's powerful, and it's here to stay.

Social media marketing is very important to enhance and support search engine optimization (SEO) efforts as once a page of a site or a link is found by social media users, it can then go 'viral' pointing many links back to the website which in turn is seen as a sign of popularity to the search genies and giving a boost in rankings to the said site.

Taking a look at the big three, as mentioned above Facebook, Twitter and YouTube we can have a look how each of these social media sites helps your marketing efforts.

Using Facebook is probably the easiest and most common social media site that people have heard of. Although Twitter has millions of users, many people only use Twitter to follow celebrities or directly for their business. The average Joe won't always be found on Twitter, whereas with Facebook as it's all about you, then a lot of people use it. Both small and large businesses rely on Facebook to help promote offers they have at the time, as well as using it to post photos and videos. It's also a great was to get people to interact as users can share updates from businesses, meaning that social media marketing is made all that much easier.

Since 2004, social media has been growing exponentially and it hasn't reached the peak of its popularity yet. There's no denying that social media platforms are now a major source of news and information. But that's not all. Social media platforms are unique in the way they interact with customers. Not only do they provide a platform for users to communicate beyond local and social boundaries, but they also offer countless possibilities to share user-generated content, like photos and videos.

But the question is, is it worth investing in social media for your business? Should social media marketing be a focus area for your marketing strategy in 2019? The answer depends on your customers, but in no way should social media marketing be ignored.

With popular social media platforms growing in terms of size, each platform has a unique audience. If you cater your content toward the audience of the social media platform, you'll be successful.

As it's the start of the year, we thought it would be a great idea to share the most important social media statistics to keep in mind for 2019. Staying on top of the latest social media statistics will help enhance your marketing strategy and plan the interactions of your business with social media.

Having a page of Facebook is the way to go for businesses and encouraging people to like it through incentives such as competitions and prizes means that people are willing to tell others about your page, and then subsequently about your business.

Twitter as mentioned above is not as all-consuming as Facebook because of the type of people using it, but if you are using Twitter to interact and make relationships and network then it is even more effective than Twitter. This is because people don't have to trawl through a page to see what you are about. What you say and do is limited to the 140 characters so you have to be clear and concise in your actions and words, therefore making it easier to impress people (or annoy them!)

Twitter takes some hard work where social media marketing is concerned as you have to build up a flowing before you can even start to influence flowers and getting that following is the start of the battle. People won't want to follow you if you constantly tweet promotional tweets or are always retweeting others messages. You have to make sure you are worthy of following and that what you say will engage people.

Once you have achieved this, then you rinse and repeat and keep writing what you have been writing that attracted your followers on the first place. Your message and business can then be spread across Twitter giving you invaluable links.

YouTube is also so commonly known that, like Twitter, you have to be very focused to successful use it in your social media marketing campaign. YouTube works more for educational websites and those selling things that could benefit from demonstrations. Using the right tags and descriptions also adds to the campaign so people can find your videos using the tags.

The videos have to be well made, and if you take the time to compile these videos and people like what they see, it can take a matter of hours for your videos to go viral, again giving you national and even international exposure!

Make sure you have a comprehensive social media marketing plan before you start and take into consideration how each of the big three sites mentioned above can enhance your business, and you won't go far wrong!

There may be many reasons. But the main reason is that man is a social animal by birth. It is our nature to be social. The internet owes it meteoric rise to this deeply human tendency to reach out and connect with another person. And, social media touches the core of another human desire - to be heard and to be involved.

Social media allows you to participate in a way that people had never imagined before. Multinational companies, which are the size of countries at times, bow down to the might of a single angry post. Our times have witnessed civil revolutions because of social media. A new breed of celebrity hood has emerged from these online platforms - Twitterati and Blogebrity to name a few.

So, is social media a juvenile and desperate offshoot of branding strategy or is it a deliberate and decisive method of increasing brand recall? Well, like always, the answer lies in the question - Do you want to be social?

Social media is all about engaging constantly. Above all things, it is a commitment to entertain honestly and inform accurately at all times and under all circumstances.

And, commitment, as you know, isn't easy. Assume that you will have many non-performing posts before you get one organic like. Prepare for nights of staring at sky-rocketing likes of other pages while your page stands at a depressing 109 likes. Get ready to be ignored and left alone from the weekend newsfeed. Know that you have to care even if they won't share.

Patience pays. And, that's why social media is important. The more you are willing to involve your audience; you will refine the ways you connect with them. You will become less of a brand, and more of a person. And, as the peeps at Forbes always say, '... people like to do business with other people, not companies. You can create brand loyalty by making more brand image more meaningful. Each day, brands like Red Bull and GoPro are thinking of cooler and smarter ways to join their consumer in their daily lives and become a part of their journey. It is a part of their well thought-out social media strategy

We will highlight a few important tips to consider as well as look at surprising statistics which should encourage business owners to step up their social media strategies.

Chapter Three

SOCIAL MEDIA AD REVENUE NUMBERS THAT MATTER!

• Instagram earns $595 million in mobile ad revenue each year. And that number only keeps increasing each year! Resource: Instagram Statistic

• Facebook earned nearly $34 billion worldwide in ad revenue in 2018! Resource: Facebook Statistic

• Twitter total ad engagements were up 91% year-over-year! Resource: Twitter Statistic

What Type of Ads are Best?

Video posts on Facebook alone get 59% more engagement than any other type of post. With that kind of reach, it's no wonder that businesses are investing more of their social marketing strategies into video ads and posts.

Live videos have become increasingly more popular and effective. Audiences love the live experience and the organic feel of "on the fly" video. Though live videos are happening 'right now', you still need to make a plan for your live video. You shouldn't script it, but have key points that you want to discuss or share with your audience.

Video Ad Statistics You Can't Ignore:

• 92% of mobile video viewers share videos with others

• 85% of the US internet audience watches video online

• Marketers who use video, grow revenue 49% faster than non-video users

• 64% of consumers make a purchase after watching branded social videos

• By 2019, internet video traffic will account for 80% of all consumer internet traffic

• Social video generates 1200% more shares than text and image content combined (G2 Crowd)

• 93% of marketers use video in their campaigns (Single Grain)

Now that you've learned how successful and important video ads are the next step is actually planning a video ad or post as part of your social media marketing strategy. But where do you start? What should you consider? Well, we've got some great tips for you!

Video Ad Tips:

• Most users scrolling through social media watch videos without the sound on. This means that you need to caption your video so your users can read the message that you are trying to get across.

• Your videos need to be exciting and captivating within the first few seconds to grab the attention of your audience.

• Video ads should be about 1-2 minutes if you're telling a story. Otherwise, keep them around 10-30 seconds. In fact, many businesses use "snack ads" which are bite-size ads of about 5-10 seconds.

• If you decide to start a live video, the biggest tip to remember is to ENGAGE with your audience! When you see users joining your live feed, welcome them by name and have mini-side conversations. Get as many users involved in the conversation. Ask questions and have them comment as you're streaming.

• Remember to keep your videos mobile-friendly as the majority of users are logged on to social media via mobile devices.

• Don't forget to stay true to your brand! Your videos should be branded so your audience will easily identify you.

• Be authentic! Drawing inspiration from other sources is completely fine but don't copy-cat exactly what another business is doing. Be you. Be your brand. Consumers are looking for authenticity among brands and the minute that they sense otherwise…they're no longer paying attention to your brand.

• Stay consistent! If you begin planning a video marketing strategy, stay consistent. Try to plan your videos for the same time and day of the week. Consumers will begin looking for that consistency especially if your video marketing is top-notch!

TIPS FOR SUCCESSFUL SOCIAL MEDIA MARKETING!

Make a plan. You can simply do a google search for "Social Media Marketing Plan" and you will hit a jackpot of useful resources. Find a plan or template that best suits your business and put it into practice. Refer to it often and tweak it as needed.

Study current trends. Social media trends and cultural trends in general change so frequently, that it's quite the task to stay in-the-know all the time. Don't get too overwhelmed, but watch and listen to what is happening and create posts and strategies that incorporate current trends.

Your customer service has to be top-notch! Customers who received great customer service will spend 21% more money on that company's products and are 71% more likely to recommend that business to others. Reply to questions and comments as swiftly as possible. Resource: Customer Service

ENGAGE! I can't stress enough how important it is for your customers to engage with you. I spend quite a bit of time looking through comments and messages and either responding to them or liking them and inviting people to like each business page if they haven't yet.

Don't engage with negative comments or reviews, but use them with your team to get better and increase your *q*uality as a business. Typically, people who complain are looking for an argument or handout and I have seen this escalate in many drawn-out conversations that just end up wasting time and causes frustration to everyone involved. Basically, just use good judgment if you decide to respond to a disgruntled customer.

If you are a retail business or restaurant, run contests and post sales or any special events that you are having. Promote, promote, promote!

Always use a photo or graphic in your posts if you're not posting a video.

Whether you have a small business and you're managing your social accounts yourself, or you're part of a large corporation with a team of social media marketers, the time to ramp up your social media strategy is now.

Chapter Four

FACEBOOK MARKETING 2019

There's no doubt that Facebook has changed the way people connect and communicate. And with the continued evolution of the platform since its 2004 launch, Facebook trends have increasingly influenced how digital marketers behave. This has made Facebook marketing as crucial an aspect of the industry as any.

Below are some of the Facebook trends you need to embrace in the coming year if you want to keep pace in the realm of Facebook marketing.

Video Will Still Be Huge

In 2018, video was the undisputed king of content. And while different variations of video emerged throughout the year (ephemeral, live, etc.), this year, and video will remain an integral part of Facebook marketing.

There are various studies and stats that back this up, but perhaps none more convincing than Mark Zuckerberg saying that Facebook users watch an average of 100 million hours of video every day. And the unfathomable amount of Facebook videos consumed has been found to get 135 percent more organic reach than photos.

These are just some of the reasons why, even though brands should already have jumped on the video bandwagon, 46 percent of marketers still plan to add Facebook video to their digital marketing plan in the coming year.

Going live

Using Facebook Live for marketing has become increasingly more important since it was rolled out to all users in April 2016. Search Engine Journal found that their average Facebook Live engagement was 178 percent higher than their average post engagement. The average reach of live posts also increased to more than double.

Facebook Live videos' organic feel (as opposed to curated ones), as well as the way it allows for real-time interactions between publishers and audiences, are a big part of why the format has been largely successful thus far.

Here are some tips on how to best leverage Facebook Live for marketing:

• Create a Facebook Event: This is a good way of making your subscribers aware of a coming Live broadcast beforehand. Similarly, you should also publish posts (across all your social media channels) in the lead up announcing the schedule of Live broadcasts, so audiences know exactly when to expect them.

• Social shares: As the broadcast is happening, schedule social shares using a consistent hashtag, so it will be easier for your followers to find the live content. You should also include the URL of your Facebook page, and tag the pertinent people/brands involved in the broadcast.

• Recap: If you plan on having regular live broadcasts, you could further increase awareness for it by publishing recap posts. Include links to the embedded videos, so those who missed out can get more of a visual clue to what went down.

The growth of AR/VR on Facebook

At its Facebook F8 2017 event, Zuckerberg made no secret of the direction they were taking AR and VR. The social media giant has never been known to stand pat, and with Camera Effects Platform, and Facebook Spaces, it's looking to lead the way towards an exciting new realm of interactions.

Camera Effects Platform

There are three key aspects of Facebook's new AR platform:

• Precise location: Precise location can place varying imagery in the camera's viewfinder. During the event, Zuckerberg showed an image of a cereal bowl with sharks swimming around it, along with a graphic saying "It's feeding time" rising from the table.

• 3D effects: The platform is designed to build out 3D environments using a 2D photo.

• Object recognition: With this, users can use real-time visuals to have new kind of interaction with images. Zuckerberg illustrated this with a photo of a plant, a wine bottle, and a mug. The plant had a thunderstorm graphic pop out to water it, while the wine bottle had an information card showing its price and origins.

In its current form, Zuckerberg admitted that it is but the next step in the evolution of AR, adding that what phone cameras can presently do are just primitive versions of what AR experiences will eventually be.

Facebook Spaces

Initially launched in Oculus Rift and Touch, this platform allows people to interact with friends (as avatars) in virtual reality.

As Facebook's promotional video shows, Spaces allows for friends to have a place to meet even if they're not in the same physical space. In the virtual world, users can share various forms of media to each other live.

What It Can Do For Marketers

As noted by Consultancy, marketers have already had a taste of what sponsored Snapchat filters can do. Facebook's Camera Effects Platform sees the former's filters, and raises the bar exponentially.

With the platform's ability to recognize any object (as opposed to just faces), there is now a myriad of creative branding possibilities. Product information will just be the tip of this new creative iceberg, with the possibility of users pointing to virtually anything (shoes, cars, clothes, food, etc.)—and have all sorts of info (and interaction) pop up. With Facebook Spaces, the platform is dependent on 360-degree content—something brands will be more than willing to provide.

It's interesting where brands will take this new available technology, but if you're going to place a bet on anything, it's on that leading brands are already exploring the vast possibilities.

Other Innovative Visual Content

GIF

If a picture paints a thousand words, then GIFs can express what words can't. And while its entertainment value has long been appreciated by netizens, brands are increasingly seeing what GIFs can do for business.

Naturally, shorter videos get more complete views. This is why GIFs have become increasingly valuable. As noted by WordStream, not only does it stand out from static images, it does not require the same amount of investment, effort-wise compared to videos, carousel, and lead ads. Additionally, you can even repurpose existing video assets as Facebook GIF ads—making it a win on repeat.

And if you need further convincing of how huge GIFs will be in 2019, according to TechCrunch, Giphy has over 200 million daily users sending 1 billion GIFs each day. It's become such huge business that Giphy runs its own studio in Los Angeles for massive clients like Nike, Paramount, McDonald's, and FOX.

Here are some tips on using GIFs for Facebook ads:

• Keep it smooth: Choppy transitions and strobing effects do not work for this format.

• Keep it simple: Trying to do too much with your GIF defeats the entire purpose of using it. Make sure that the message you're trying to relay, the transitions, and the CTAs are as simple as possible.

• Use as part of a strategy: Sure, some GIFs just have that viral magic about them, but you can't count on yours being one of them. Instead of trying to create magic, use GIF ads as a complementary part of a series of visual content. Make sure you understand how to use GIFs before aiming to make it your main strategy.

Press and hold videos

If you haven't encountered a photo with a CTA to press and hold, then chances are you're an Android user. The feature (only

46

available for iOS users), basically allows people to physically press a photo before taking them to either a video or an image slideshow. When they lift their fingers off the screen, they're taken back to the static photo (here's a guide on how to make one).

What it can do for marketers

Engagement is the name of the game when it comes to Facebook marketing, and this format allows you to interact with audiences in real time right on their newsfeeds. Because the format is still relatively new, you can surprise your subscribers with interesting content—at least while its novelty lasts.

360 Photos/Videos

Considered by some to be a form of VR, 360-degree media keeps right in line with the need to create more immersive brand experiences. And because most of the leading brands will continually increase their pivot to video, you're going to have to find a way to stand out from what will inevitably become white video noise.

What It Can Do For Marketers

Anthony Holland Parkin, head of VR at Getty Images, notes that technological advancements in 360-degree cameras have provided brands with the tools to tell stories from new vantage points. He cited people going to social media during Fashion Week to have a real-time look at next season's trends.

Another possibility Parkin points out, which could be developed in the future, is the ability to purchase an item within a 360-degree media experience.

Continuous Rise Of Chatbots

According to Facebook, there are now 100,000 monthly active bots on Messenger, providing an instant connection between brands and customers. Customer service remains the main realm of chatbots, addressing basic queries and issues, and providing an automated interaction to drive sales.

Here are some tips for creating chatbots:

• Create a character first: Chatbots are meant to feel personal, and as such, you need to think of a persona first before focusing on the code.

• Keep it simple: You want to acclimate your customers to the technology. One way to drive them away from chatbots is by making the process too complicated. Keep it simple, and give them a reason to use it.

• It won't be perfect: Customer service is always tricky, and you're never going to get it perfectly— whether it's a human or a bot.

Takeaway

The development of new technologies has birthed more creative possibilities for brands to engage and interact with their customers. And with Facebook making the integration of these innovations to its platform as seamless as can be, marketers need to jump at the opportunities to stay ahead of the competition.

Which of these trends can you integrate into your Facebook marketing strategy? Experiment with some of these elements, and test how it works. It could lead to the spark your brand needs to stand out.

PAID FACEBOOK MARKETING

As of September 2018, more than 2.2 billion people are using Facebook.

That huge, global audience means Facebook is a key marketing platform for just about every business. But the ever-changing Facebook algorithm can make it a challenge to connect organically with fans. That's where Facebook ads come in. With micro-targeting features that allow you to reach your exact target audience based on demographics, location, interests, and even behaviors. You can always get your message in front of the people who are most likely to want your products or services.

Facebook offers a variety of paid ad options and placements, but all ads can be broken down into three elements:

• Campaigns. The campaign houses all of your assets.

• Ad sets. If you're targeting separate audiences with different characteristics, you'll need an individual ad set for each.

• Ads. Your actual ads live within your ad sets. Each ad set can hold a variety of ads that vary in color, copy, images, etc.

With that terminology out of the way, let's dive in to creating an ad.

Start creating an ad through Facebook's Ads Manager.

You can create a paid ad on Facebook using Facebook's Ads Manager.

Once you log into this page, you'll see a performance dashboard where all of your campaigns, ad sets, and ads will be listed including the results they've driven for your Facebook page. Unless you've already created an ad for your Facebook page, this dashboard will be empty.

Choose an objective.

Facebook's Ads Manager, like many social media advertising networks, is designed with your campaign objective in mind. Before getting started, Ads Manager will prompt you to choose an objective for your campaign:

Choose An Objective.

Facebook's Ads Manager, like many social media advertising networks, is designed with your campaign objective in mind. Before getting started, Ads Manager will prompt you to choose an objective for your campaign:

There are 11 different objectives to choose from. The list includes everything from general brand awareness, to getting installs of your app, to increasing traffic to your online store.

By choosing one of these objectives, you're giving Facebook a better idea of what you'd like to do so they can present you with the best-suited ad options. As shown in the screenshot above, Facebook's ad options include:

- Brand awareness
- Reach
- Website traffic
- Engagement
- App installs
- Video views
- Lead generation
- Messages
- Conversions
- Catalog sales
- Store traffic

Let's say, for sake of this blog post, you're looking to drive more traffic to your website. When you select this option, Facebook will prompt you to enter the URL you're looking to promote. If you're using marketing automation software, be sure to create a unique tracking URL with UTM parameters for this to ensure that you'll be able to keep track of traffic and conversions from this ad. For Hub Spot customers, this can be done using the Tracking URL Builder.

Once selected, Facebook will then display the ad option that makes the most sense in terms of achieving this objective.

Choose Your Audience.

Your next step is to configure your target audience -- you can do this for each ad set that belongs to the same campaign. If you're just starting out with paid advertising on Facebook, it's likely that you'll have to experiment with several different targeting options until you reach an audience that fits just right. To help you narrow your focus, Facebook's targeting criteria are accompanied by an audience definition gauge. This tool -- located to the right of the audience targeting fields -- takes all of your selected properties into consideration in order to come up with a potential reach number.

If you're wavering between choosing a specific audience over a broad one, consider your objective. If you're looking to drive traffic, you'll probably want to focus on the type of people you know will be interested in your offering. However, if you're looking to build brand awareness or promote a widely appealing offer, feel free to focus on a more general audience.

Facebook's built-in targeting is vast, including options such as:

• Location

- Age

- Gender

- Languages

- Relationship

- Education

- Work

- Financial

- Home

- Ethnic Affinity

- Generation

- Parents

- Politics (U.S. only)

- Life Events

- Interests

- Behaviors

- Connections

You also have the option to select a Custom Audience -- this allows you to target people on Facebook who are in your company's contact database, visited a page on your website that has a tracking pixel, or use your app or game. To learn more about how to set up an Custom Audience on Facebook, check out these instructions. (And for more on the specifics of these criteria, visit this Facebook targeting resource.)

Once you find a group that responds well to your ads, Facebook allows you to save these audiences to be used again later -- so you may not need to dive into this step once you've been running Facebook ads for a while.

Set Your Budget.

Facebook allows you to set either a daily budget or a lifetime budget. Here's how they differ from each other:

• Daily budget. If you want your ad set to run continuously throughout the day, this is the option you'll want to go for. Using a daily budget means that Facebook will pace your spending per day. Keep in mind that the minimum daily budget for an ad set is $1.00 USD and must be at least 2X your CPC.

• Lifetime budget. If you're looking to run your ad for a specified length of time, select lifetime budget. This means Facebook will pace your spend over the time period you set for the ad to run.

To further specify your budgeting, turn to the advanced options -- this option is linked at the bottom of the screenshot shown above. This section allows you to specify a few things:

Schedule

Choose whether or not your want your campaign to run immediately and continuously or if you want to customize the start and end dates. You can also set parameters so that your ads only run during specific hours and days of the week.

Optimization & Pricing

Choose whether or not you want to bid for your objective, clicks, or impressions. (This will alter how your ad is displayed and paid for.) By doing so, you'll pay for your ad to be shown to people within your target audience that are more likely to complete your desired action, but Facebook will control what your maximum bid is.

If you don't want Facebook to set optimal bids for you, you'll want to opt for manual bidding. This option awards you full control over how much you're willing to pay per action completed. However, Facebook will provide a suggested bid based on other advertisers' behavior to give you a sense of what you should shoot for.

Delivery

Delivery type falls under two categories: standard and accelerated. Standard delivery will show your ads throughout the day, while accelerated delivery helps you reach an audience quickly for time-sensitive ads (Note: this option requires manual bid pricing).

Create Your Ad.

What do you want your ad to look like? It all depends on your original objective.

If you're looking to increase the number of clicks to your website, Facebook's Ad Manager will suggest the Clicks to Website ad options. Makes sense, right?

This ad option is broken down into two formats: Links and Carousels. Essentially, this means that you can either display a single image ad (Links) or a multi-image ad (Carousel) with three to five scrolling images at no additional cost.

Once you decide between the two, you'll need to upload your creative assets. It's important to note that for each type of ad, Facebook requires users to adhere to certain design criteria.

For single image ads, Facebook asks that users adhere to the following design recommendations:

• Text: 125 characters

• Ad Headline: 25 characters

• Image ratio: 1.91:1

• Image resolution (including CTA): 1080 x 1080 pixels

For multi-image ads -- also known as Carousel Ads -- Facebook provides the following design recommendations:

• Recommended image size: 1080 x 1080 pixels

• Image ratio: 1:1

• Text: 125 characters

• Headline: 40 characters

• Link description: 20 characters

Your image may not include more than 20% text. See how much text is on your image.

Keep in mind that these are the ad options for the "Traffic" objective.

If you selected "boost your posts," you'd be presented with different ad options like the Page Post Engagement: Photo ad. This ad has a unique set of design recommendations.

Once you select an ad type, the Ads Manager will prompt you to identify how you'd like to display your ad. The options they provide are as follows: Desktop News Feed, Mobile News Feed, and Desktop Right Column.

Here's how each ad would appear:

* Desktop News Feed

* Mobile News Feed

* Desktop Right Column

Be aware if your ad isn't associated with a Facebook page, you'll only be able to run Desktop Right Column ads. To leverage all three display locations, you can learn how to create a Facebook Page here.

Report On Your Ads' Performance.

Once your ads are running, you'll want to keep an eye on how they're doing. To see their results, you'll want to look in two places: the Facebook Ad Manager and your marketing software.

Facebook's Ad Manager

Facebook's Ad Manager is a sophisticated dashboard that provides users with an overview of all their campaigns.

Upfront, the dashboard highlights an estimate of how much you're spending each day. The dashboard is organized by columns, which makes it easy to filter through your ads so you can create a custom view of your results. Key numbers like reach, frequency, and cost are readily available, making reporting on performance a no brainer.

According to Facebook, here are some of the key metrics to look for (and their definitions):

• Performance. Can be customized further to include metrics like results, reach, frequency and impressions

• Engagement. Can be customized further to include metrics like Page likes, Page engagement and post engagement

• Videos. Can be customized further to include metrics like video views and avg. % of video viewed

• Website. Can be customized further to include metrics like website actions (all), checkouts, payment details, purchases and adds to cart

• Apps. Can be further customized to include metrics like app installs, app engagement, credit spends, mobile app actions and cost per app engagement

• Events. Can be further customized to include metrics like event responses and cost per event response

• Clicks. Can be further customized to include metrics like clicks, unique clicks, CTR (click-through rate) and CPC (cost per click)

• Settings. Can be further customized to include metrics like start date, end date, ad set name, ad ID, delivery, bid and objective

Your Marketing Software

While there are certainly a lot of details to keep straight when planning a paid Facebook ad, it's important that you don't lose sight of the big picture. Reporting on clicks and conversions from Facebook is important; however, if you're using URLs with specific UTM codes, you have an opportunity to measure your ads' full-funnel effectiveness using your marketing software.

Tracking URLs will help your marketing software keep track of how many leads, or better yet, how many customers you've gained from your advertising efforts. This information is useful in determining the ROI of this source, and can also be used to inform your overall Facebook marketing strategy.

FACEBOOK MARKETING TIPS 2019

Facebook is a global powerhouse when it comes to social media marketing. It was the first social network to release ads and although most other social networks would never admit it, Facebook set the standard for how ads are run on social networks. It comes as no surprise that many businesses depend on Facebook for their marketing needs. Of course, just like any marketing platform, Facebook has its ups and downs. Just recently, Facebook began reducing the influence of business ads on newsfeed to bolster social interaction and meaningful connections. You can check the Facebook Newsroom if you wish to learn more about the matter.

Despite the recent changes, Facebook is still the top social media network for businesses looking to expand their reach. According to "Statista," there are over 2.234 billion monthly active Facebook users from all over the world as of the second quarter of 2018. . No other social network can pull off these kinds of numbers. Still, given the recent challenges, it is more important than ever for businesses to ensure that they are doing Facebook marketing right if only to make the most out of what the social network has to offer in terms of promoting one's product or service.

Here are ten tips that you can implement in your Facebook marketing strategy to promote and grow your business.

1. Make Sure That You Have The Right Business Page On Facebook

You need a proper business page and not a personal profile to market a business on Facebook effectively. This might seem obvious, but many social media consultants are often surprised how many marketers get this part wrong. Also, you need to make sure that your Facebook business page falls under the right classification from the following six types:

• Local business or place
• Artist, band or public figure
• Company, organization or institution
• Entertainment
• Brand or product
• Cause or community

Choosing the right category is vital as specific features may or may not be available to you should you choose the wrong category? For example, selecting "local business or place" gives you an option to set a physical address while categories like "Brand or product" lacks that feature.

2. Optimize Your Images

You need to make sure that you put up some quality images on your Facebook business page. Social networks can be extremely visual and more when you are doing Facebook marketing. From the profile picture, cover photos and updates — all images should be as captivating as possible and convey to people what it is that your business does.

3. Use The CTA (Call To Action) Button

Another feature that many marketers tend to overlook when doing online marketing agency through the Facebook social network is to include a simple CTA button on every business page. If you do not have one throughout your website, then you are leaving a significant amount of money on the table.

What the CTA button says and does depend entirely on how you set it up and you have no shortage of options — Shop Now, Sign Up, Contact Us, Use App, See Video and more. You can connect these buttons to your landing page, a contact form, a video that you would like to promote or an opt-in page. It all depends on what you are looking to accomplish with your Facebook business page.

4. Start regularly posting "balanced" content

Now that you have your Facebook business page in order, it is time to create content for users. Do not limit yourself to just one type of content and embrace the opportunity to experiment with different formats to see which combination your audience likes best.

If you are finding it difficult to mix up your content and engaging your audience, you can always start with the 70-20-10 habit:

• publish original material 70 percent of the time

• post content relevant to the interest of your audience 20 percent of the time

• Create self-promotional content only 10 percent of the time

If you go by the rules mentioned above, you would be able to mix up your content and never run into the problem of boring your audience. More importantly, it opens up an opportunity to voice our concerns and express your observations in your niche.

5. Optimize Your Posts

The Facebook Newsfeed can be a very crowded space for businesses to do any marketing. How you craft your posts will either make them stand out or send them straight into the bottom of the Newsfeed Ocean never to be seen again? Updates from Facebook business pages accompanied by high quality and compelling images are up to 10 times more effective in producing audience engagement compared to posts that only have plain text.

If the purpose of your social media update is to share a link, make sure that you eliminate the link URL from the post. To do so, simply paste the link and give Facebook a few seconds to capture the information about the URL (image, title, and first paragraph) and then delete the URL before posting. Doing so will help make your post appear less cluttered and help drive focus to the subject and image of your post. If you must share link outside of what

Facebook provides, you can use Google URL Shortener to make the job look cleaner and more shareable.

6. Leverage User-Generated Content

In Facebook marketing, you do not have to create your content all the time. Every once in a while, you can share content created by your audience. Doing so not only saves you time and effort but likewise help promote brand loyalty as you make users feel appreciated that they are contributing to your cause.

Among the most straightforward methods to obtain user-generated content is to ask users to share photos of their experience with your product or service. You can also share posts on your community page when one of your fans or followers mentions your business. Most people love recognition even when it is on social media with their favorite brands taking the time to thank and feature them.

7. Post Videos More Often

Another great way to increase engagement in social media is through videos. Users watch over 100 million hours of video on Facebook on a daily basis, and that is only the beginning. Facebook is also making adjustments to how their algorithm determines individual interest through the videos that users are watching.

There are some essential things to bear in mind when you're producing videos for Facebook:

• 85% of Facebook users prefer watching videos on mute. This implies that captioning your videos will be vital to engagement.

• 80% of users are irritated when videos auto-plays on their newsfeed, so make sure that you're setting up your videos correctly when you post.

• Take advantage of "Facebook Live" if you are not keen on producing your videos. The latter is a streaming service that lets you broadcast live videos straight from your smartphone. Many businesses have found that it is an excellent way to create leads and maximize engagement.

8. Use Facebook Page Insights To Monitor Progress

Regular Facebook updates are only half the battle. The other half is about monitoring your metrics to discover trends in engagement so that you know exactly what you are doing right (and what you are doing wrong). The best tool for this job is Facebook's internal analytics tool called the Facebook Page Insights.

Page Insights provides users with a clear picture of how your business page was doing over the last week with details of the following:

• number of page likes/unlikes

• Post Reach

• Engagement

• Comments

• Shares

9. Time Your Posts Correctly

You should also consider the timing of your Facebook posts. Not many people realize this, but there is such a thing as the most opportune time when posting updates as opposed to just randomly dropping content on your Facebook page. So how do you do just that?

You can get information on the best times to publish a Facebook post via your Page Insights screen. To access this feature, click on the "Insights" tab at the top of your Facebook business page.

The Insights screen shows you everything that you need to know to time your posts correctly which includes the following:

• The time when most of your Facebook followers are online

• How well a particular piece of content does throughout the day

• Information on which of your posts is creating the most engagement.

You can use the information mentioned above to get insights on the best time to engage your users. You might attempt to publish various materials (casual humor posts, and so on) at different times of the day to see how it affects engagement. By learning the best time to post, you can maximize reach for just about everything that you do when marketing your business on Facebook.

10. Take Advantage Of Audience Insights

Last but not least on the list of analytics tools that you can use for Facebook marketing is Audience Insights. As the name suggests, Audience Insights gives you details about your users. All you need to do is pick an audience and the page provides you demographics such as age, gender, level of education and profession. Such information can prove useful for uncovering the interest and hobbies of your target audience. As a result, you will have a good idea of what topics and type of content most of your audience find intriguing.

No matter how much Facebook may change its algorithms, one thing is for sure — the social network will remain to be a viable marketing platform for many years to come. The key to success is to keep on improving your approach, and you can start with the tips mentioned above and make sure that you have everything covered.

Chapter Five

INSTAGRAM MARKETING 2019

When Instagram first popped onto the scene back in 2010, it was just like any other social platform: filled with selfies, pets, and pictures of food. Fast-forward to 2019 and Instagram's transformation from a simple photo sharing app to a full-on marketing channel is nearly complete.

Just look at some of the platform's newest features! In the last year alone, Instagram has released dozens of new tool for businesses, including advanced analytics, shoppable Instagram posts, and new ways to drive traffic from Instagram Stories, and the new standalone video platform, IGTV.

If you think Instagram is just for sunsets, selfies, and staged shots of food, you are sorely mistaken.

With Facebook at its helm, the number of active users growing every month, and 85% of top brands adopting the social platform as an avenue for reaching their audience, there is no better time than now for your company to get on board with Instagram as a marketing platform for your business.

There are over 600 million active monthly users on Instagram, over 95 million photos and videos are shared each day and those images and videos garner more than 4.2 billion "likes."

Imagine if your posts were able to generate even a fraction of that kind of engagement. With users so actively involved with your brand, you have a greater opportunity to reach and be heard by them, and ultimately, generate more sales.

Whether you work in ecommerce, education, or media and publishing, it pays to build a presence on Instagram. But if you really want to get ahead, you need to know the platform (and your audience) inside and out, including what kind of content resonates most, how to build an Instagram Stories strategy, and how to track your metrics and KPIs.

That's where this guide comes in:

• The fundamentals of a well-rounded Instagram marketing strategy

• Tips on how to create an effective Instagram profile

- Running your first Instagram influencer marketing campaign
- The ins and outs of your Instagram analytics
- Tips on how to use Instagram Stories for business
- And so much more!

But first, let's take a look at why Instagram marketing is so effective for ecommerce businesses in particular.

WHY INSTAGRAM MARKETING IS KEY TO ECOMMERCE SUCCESS

We all know how great Instagram is for sharing photos and videos with our friends and family, but it's also an incredible channel for ecommerce marketing. But why?

Well, an obvious reason is Instagram's format. Because of this visual nature, Instagram holds massive opportunities for ecommerce businesses looking to showcase their products. Whether through regular photos, videos, or Instagram Stories, millions of businesses have learned that building a visual presence on Instagram can hugely compliment their ecommerce marketing.

There's also the fact that Instagram users are more engaged than the average social media user. And while trends do seem to show that Instagram engagement is dropping (something we'll be discussing in the next chapter), the platform is still producing higher engagement rates for businesses compared to both Twitter and Facebook.

But Instagram users are more than simply engaged -- they're also commonly online shoppers. According to a recent study, 72% of Instagram users report making a purchase decision after seeing something on Instagram, with the most popular categories being clothing, makeup, shoes, and jewelry. This shopping mindset makes Instagram users the perfect audience because they're high-intent and quick to convert.

Another reason Instagram is so great for ecommerce has to do with the platform itself. As we mentioned in the previous chapter, Instagram has recently introduced a ton of new business-facing tools -- and there's definitely more to come! Whether through links in Instagram Stories or shoppable Instagram posts, soon enough many of our online shopping experiences will start (and end) on Instagram.

All of this said, it would be a mistake to think that just because you don't sell ecommerce products your business doesn't belong on Instagram! Beyond its unique ability to move products, Instagram is also an incredible place for businesses to build brand awareness and connect with new audiences (and potential customers).

Instagram Analytics

In order to truly maximize your business' Instagram presence, you need to know what's working, what you're doing well, and where you're seeing results. Given the few options you have for driving direct referral traffic from Instagram, this will largely come down to measuring your on-platform analytics, and keeping a close eye on what's generating audience engagement and helping to build your presence.

But it does seem, at least at this stage, that marketers are not totally sold on Instagram's own analytics options.

In response to the question 'How useful do you find Instagram's native analytics data for your strategic planning?', the majority indicated that they're only 'Somewhat' useful for their purposes.

Instagram offers a range of analytics options for business profiles, including location insights, gender, and when your followers are active. Those are all clearly valuable, but the responses here would suggest that businesses are looking for more.

Some third party tools offer various other elements which can help in strategic planning, and it is possible that Instagram will look to add more functionality in future. Facebook Page Insights, for example, offers a broader set of information, and given they're owned by the same company, you would expect that Instagram, too, would look to get up to similar speed.

That would clearly be beneficial – respondents highlighted several key issues with the current Instagram analytics offerings, including the lack of desktop functionality for the analytics suite, the need for more hashtag insights (in terms of which are driving visitors to their profiles and content), and downloadable data formats for expanded investigation.

But the most requested addition for Instagram analytics was, by far, the expansion of the data period to enable more in-depth trend tracking. While having an overview of current trends is valuable, being able to identify key shifts and changes over longer periods is key to developing an optimal platform strategy. Instagram's current analytics are limited in this respect, leaving marketers with a lot of manual data tracking – if Instagram were able to improve on this, it would make things a lot easier for those looking to optimize their performance.

The Do's and Don'ts of Using Instagram for Business in 2019

Here are some of the essential dos and don'ts of using Instagram for marketing your business in 2019.

Do Post Regularly

As with any social network, if you're going to bother with having a brand presence, you need to commit to at least posting regularly to your account. Having an Instagram account with nothing on it -- or with no posts for weeks or months -- is worse than having no account at all.

How many times should you post to Instagram per day?

Consistency is key with Instagram. Data shows that brands that post between two and 10 times per day get the best results with their Instagram marketing efforts.

The exact number of posts that you make should depend upon how much you have to say. Better to post fewer updates with great photos and videos than a larger volume that aren't going to capture the interest of your audience.

Do Interact With Your Customers

While limited in features, compared to other social networks, Instagram still enables you to interact with your customers through:

• Likes

• Comments

• Private messages

• Regrams

Instagram itself does a great job with this. They interact with their users via the "weekend hashtag project" (WHP). If you follow their account, you know that every weekend, the team challenges their community by asking users to create photos around a designated theme, with the incentive being a chance at getting featured as one of their favorites on their profile throughout the week.

Another way your business could generate photos and interact with your audience is by creating a dedicated hashtag where users can share their photos with you. Ultra Beauty does this by including the hashtag #ultabeauty in their bio.

Do Get Your Customers Involved in Content Creation

There is really no better way to create engagement with your brand than to encourage your customers to create content for it. User-Generated Content (UGC) is authentic and shows loyalty to your brand, so capitalize on it!

Consider creating a unique hashtag, asking your followers to post a photo using it, and then posting your favorites to your brand's account. By doing this, fans will feel more connected to your brand, you'll create buzz and engagement, and perhaps their content will help you to generate your next big idea.

A great example of a brand that routinely leverages UGC for its marketing is ipsy, a purveyor of personalized monthly makeup and beauty product subscription boxes.

They've created a vibrant community on Instagram where "ipsters" can creatively show off goodies from their subscription box along with their ideas and experiences with them. The brand then regularly re-grams their favorites, tagging the user, and giving them their fifteen minutes of fame.

Do Invest in High-Quality Images that Tell a Story

Images are key to helping you tell a story -- especially on an almost entirely visual platform like Instagram. In order for you to effectively tell your story, you can't use any old photos. They need to be authentic and original. Instagram isn't the place for stock photos. Consider sharing the login information to your account with members of your team so that they can share their photos as soon as something memorable happens (but do also set guidelines around what can -- and cannot -- be posted on your brand account).

If you follow HubSpot on Instagram, you've probably noticed that they regularly feature their employees with #hubspotemployeetakeover and #humansofhubspot. Not only do you get an inside look at their team, but also their culture and office.

Providing your audience with a story like this will keep them coming back daily by adding a more personal connection to the relationship they have with your brand. They want to know about your company, but also the people behind it.

Do Use Video

Over the years, Instagram has added and made significant improvements to their video features.

Extend your brand's storytelling experience by using video to capture funny team moments, walk people through your office, highlight how a product works, or create a tutorial.

Video doesn't only have to be for funny cat videos or musicians.

Unlike an introductory video or longer form videos typically uploaded to YouTube, Instagram's 60-sec video limit allows your company to create content that is fun and informational without losing your viewer's interest.

If you're going to create a video for Instagram, remember to use a tripod and avoid background noise. Because Instagram is inherently a visual platform, the quality of your visuals matters.

Do Direct People to Your Bio

Your bio is prime real estate for telling users what to do and where to go. Use those precious 150 characters to create a strong call-to-action and guide people.

One major difference between Instagram and other social platforms like Facebook, Twitter and LinkedIn, is that it doesn't allow links in comments or captions. As a result, the link in your bio is your only chance to get people to click through and visit your website.

Use your Instagram posts to tease an offer then direct them to the link in your bio to follow through. Make it a practice to tell users how they can sign up or purchase something by clicking on the link in your bio. It's common to see brands change this link frequently as they share a photo with a new offer.

Do Consider Instagram Sponsored Ads

Since it was acquired by Facebook, Instagram ads are far more comprehensive than they ever have been. If you are a particularly visual brand or market a product, consider using these to get in front of more potential customers.

Not only will it expand the reach of your post (and bypass the algorithm), but it will enable you to link users directly from your photo or video.

Do Use Hashtags, but Don't Spam

As we mentioned above, hashtags can be a great way to engage with and get found by your audience but do not abuse them.

While Instagram allows users much more freedom than Twitter and their strict character count, it's important to use hashtags that are specific to your brand or relevant to your industry or image. #Catsofinstagram will get you in front of a lot of people, but you probably don't want to use it unless a friendly feline will be making an appearance.

Don't Use Instagram Solely For Promotion

You should never over promote on any social network, but use extra caution on Instagram. It may be tempting to post a lot of product photos or ads you'd regularly see in the sidebar of a website, but try to avoid this. People on Instagram are looking for beautiful, striking images, not sales pitches. If you are going to use Instagram Ads (the platform's official paid advertisements) make sure that your content is targeted to your audience and still feels natural.

Be creative, and post pictures and videos users will want to engage with.

Don't Post Generic Or Stock Photographs

You want your brand to have some personality on Instagram. Don't post generic pictures that look to be carefully staged (i.e. a formal headshot). Show a little bit of a wild side. Take pictures that show your brand's personality and office culture. You don't want to come off like a stick in the mud on Instagram.

PAID INSTAGRAM MARKETING

According to Forrester research, Instagram has about 10x the interaction with a brand, as a percentage of the brand's fans or followers that Facebook does. Instagram has an even more substantial lead on the other social networks.

This gives great opportunities for brands wanting to communicate with their followers.

In partial compensation for Instagram's enhanced engagement, it is likely to cost you more to place your ad there than it would on Facebook

But the difference in price between a Facebook ad and Instagram one is nowhere near the difference in engagement between the two platforms. This means that although you may end up paying more to advertise on Instagram, you are likely to end up with better results overall.

AdEspresso analyzed Facebook and Instagram ads in 2016. They found that the average cost to advertise on Instagram (in terms of CPC) was $0.70. This is double Facebook's average CPC of $0.35.

Remembering that Instagram often has up to 10 times the engagement of Facebook, you are likely to get far better results from your ads.

Costs will vary by market, however. For instance, fewer business people spend time on Instagram so Instagram B2B costs can be high.

Key Factors Contributing To Advertising Cost

As with Facebook advertising, three main factors affect what you will have to pay for your Instagram ads:

• The amount you are willing to bid for your campaign

• Your ads' Relevance Score –how relevant Facebook / Instagram considers your advertisements in relation to the people you are trying to serve your ads to

• Your Estimated Action Rates – how likely that Facebook / Instagram believes that people will take the action for which you target your ads, e.g., how likely are people to convert when they see your ad?

Facebook explains these factors in more detail in their Help section.

A crucial factor from this is that your Instagram advertising price is not affected by your bid alone. You can reduce your advertising costs by creating quality ads that people will value, and focusing your ads on the most suitable people.

Creating Your Instagram Ads In The Most Cost-Effective Way

Too many people place ads on Instagram (and often Facebook) without knowing what they are doing. It should be no surprise, therefore, that these people often lose money. You need to think carefully about the people you are targeting and create the perfect ad for these people.

Facebook / Instagram split its Ads Manager into three sections:

• Campaign

• Ad Set

• Ad

They allow you to build your ads up following these three parts:

1. Set Campaign Details

You begin by selecting your objective for your entire Instagram Marketing Campaign

There is no value going into this process without knowing what you wish to gain out of it. You need to begin your campaign by setting campaign goals and objectives.

The Facebook / Instagram Ads Manager offer you 11 different marketing objectives in three categories:

Awareness

• Brand Awareness

• Reach

Consideration

• Traffic

• Engagement

• App Installs

• Video Views

• Lead Generation

• Messages

Conversion

• Conversions

• Catalogue Sales

• Store Visits

Make sure you don't select an irrelevant objective for Instagram – for instance focusing on Messages (which is designed for those wanting to get more people to send messages to your business in Messenger).

If you are just beginning your advertising on Instagram, it is a good idea to optimize for conversions. Instagram will target your campaigns to give you your best results at a lower price.

2. Set Details for Your Ad Set

You may have various settings to choose from, depending on your preferred objective. For instance, if you opt to focus on increasing traffic you are asked whether you want to target a website, app, or Messenger. You are then asked whether you want to create an offer to help encourage people to convert, depending on your objective. You are then given the opportunity to define your audience. If you want the best price for your ads and the best ROI on them, you want to be smart and create a selected audience. You are given quite a few options for targeting your ads, and you can save your audiences so that they can be reused in future campaigns.

Don't waste money by broad targeting. You might think that you will have a higher chance of converting if 10 million people see your ad – but the majority of these people have no wish to buy anything from you.

You can target based on:

• Location

• Age

• Gender

• Languages

• Demographics

• Interests

• Behaviors

• Connections

Facebook / Instagram will give you an indication of your estimated daily reach and expected post engagement. They will indicate whether you have targeted your audience specifically or broadly.

You then choose your placements. This is where you select to focus your advertising on Instagram, rather than Facebook. You will need to deselect Automatic Placements and instead opt for Edit Placements. Amongst the options you encounter are Instagram Feed and Instagram Stories. The device type doesn't matter as you can't select Instagram for Desktop.

It is a good idea to do this even if you want to do a combined campaign involving Facebook, too. By selecting your placements yourself, you have more control over your campaign optimization.

You have a few other options here; for instance, you can choose to target all mobile devices, or just iOS or Android.

Finally, in the Ad Set section, you provide your budget. You can either pick a daily budget limit or give a total Lifetime Budget amount for your entire ad set.

When you set a daily budget, you create an average, rather than an absolute limit. This is particularly important if you choose to set a budget based on an action. Instagram may be able to control the number of times they serve ads (thus limiting the impressions you have to pay for). But it is harder for them to manage how many times people click on a particular day. There are days where many people may click. If you have CPC pricing, you will go over your budget that day, but Instagram will try and compensate tomorrow.

You also have the chance to state the timeframe in which you want your ads to run.

You also have a few options to optimize your ad delivery. For instance, you can choose whether you want your Instagram ad to run multiple times per day to a person, or just the once. You can select what kind of optimizations you wish for ad delivery. For instance, you can ask Instagram to concentrate on delivering your ads to people most likely to click on a link or view a landing page. You may ask them to show your ads to as many people (within your defined audience) as possible, and focus on impressions.

You also define the method by which Facebook / Instagram charges you, e.g., are you paying cost per click (CPC), or by impressions (CPM), or by another metric?

You also have the option to select Manual or Automatic Bidding. Many people recommend that newcomers go with Automatic Bidding, but you may prefer to bid manually once you are experienced with advertising on Instagram. If you opt for Manual Bidding you have a further choice to make: should you set Maximum or Average bids?

If you select Maximum bid, then Instagram won't run your ads if the cost per result would be higher than your bid. You would choose this if your goal is to maximize profit.

If you select Average bid, Instagram optimizes your ad delivery to maximize your ROI – they call this the Pacing method. The Pacing method ensures that you don't use up your entire budget early in the day, and miss out on profitable opportunities later in the day. You would select the Average bid if you want to maximize delivery, i.e., you would get more conversions, but some may cost more than what would otherwise have been your maximum bid. You should probably begin with automatic bidding until you can build up data showing your cost per result.

One common suggestion the experts make is that if you opt for Manual bidding, select a figure towards the bottom end of Facebook's suggested bid range.

3. Set Details Relating to Your Specific Ads

This section focuses on your actual Instagram ads.

Your first option is to select an ad format. You can choose from:

• Carousel

• Single Image

• Single Video

• Slideshow

Note that the option of Collection is currently only available for the Mobile Facebook feed – not Instagram.

If you aim to advertise using Instagram Stories you can select from:

- Instagram Stories Single Image

- Instagram Stories Single Video

If you want to keep your ad costs down, carousel ads are typically seen as providing the best value for your money.

Once you select the format for your ad, you provide all of the other details necessary to create the ad. These include any links, images, and videos – as well as the all-important Call to Action text.

Native Ads Work Best On Instagram

Instagram users expect to receive relevant, interesting posts. They can spot a traditional ad, and these perform poorly. If you want your ad to work on Instagram, it needs to look like a typical post. This means that may not receive the best results from the ads with the lowest CPM. Your ad may not cost you much to deliver. But that is of little value to you if everybody bypasses it.

It is essential that you create content that your target audience appreciates. Don' try and push sales with your first ads. It is better to begin by creating top-of-funnel posts, to introduce your brand to the people who you are targeting. Instagram recognizes this too. Your Relevance Score is an excellent guide as to how well you target your content.

Instagram is one of the fastest-growing social networks. Two years ago, few people included Instagram in their top echelon of social networks. Now it is considered one of the leading players.

Most firms who advertise online, or work with influencers, who assist them in their marketing, should give serious consideration to including Instagram in their marketing mix.

INSTAGRAM MARKETING TIPS 2019

According to Forrester, Instagram has more than 1 billion monthly active users with 50% following brands. In addition, audience engagement is at 4.21% which is higher than other social media channels. Given these statistics, it is up to businesses to capitalize and use the channel to market their business. In this article, we shall take a look at some tips on how to leverage Instagram for marketing your business.

1. Know How Often To Post

Being active to build engagement and attract followers is the name of the game in Instagram marketing. But you do not have to overdo it. According to studies 1-2 posts daily is enough. Knowing the best time to post is critical in Instagram especially when dealing with the network's algorithmic timeline. Posting time may vary depending on the market you want to target.

2. Don't Preach, Tell A Story Instead

When marketing in Instagram, you need to remember that it is a "visual inspiration platform." Attract attention with images and videos. Tell a story to increase audience engagement. Tell micro-stories using captions, videos, Instagram Stories and profile.

3. Make Your Branding Count

When sending your message, make sure that it is clear, creative, and consistent. Utilizing an erratic and haphazard approach will not work. Focus on your core activities such as profile presentation, creating style patterns, and master hashtag use. React to Instagram comments regularly to build engagement and customer loyalty.

4. Utilize The Full Range Of Instagram Video Formats

Pictures have been the stalwart Instagram. Over the years, however, it has added video capability to its fold. Pictures can reach thousands of potential customers but videos can reach 1.8 million. As a business, you cannot challenge the effectiveness of online videos. Take advantage of Instagram's video options for your marketing campaigns. You can create a single ad by combining videos and stills.

5. Use Video Subtitles And Closed Captions

Although videos have dominated the online space, many potential customers prefer switching off audio and just watch the video. For this reason, you should make use of subtitles and captions to deliver your message alongside your videos. Research by Facebook revealed that captions can increase video view times by 12%. The effectiveness of your message will also increase by 82% compared to 18% with audio and no captions.

6. Take Advantage Of Instagram Video Ad Formats

With 75% of Instagram users declaring that they take action such as visiting sites, searching, or recommending to a friend after reading a post, take the time to master Instagram's range of advertisement formats. While photos remain the bread and butter of Instagram, video advertising has gained popularity in the platform in the last few years. There are three video formats you can take advantage of in Instagram namely single video ads, carousel, and Instagram Stories.

7. Give Gifs A Try

Research reveals that more people watch the tail end of videos that are less than 15 seconds. This is where learning how to create and post GIF will come in handy for your marketing campaign. GIFs are more appealing than photos. They are shared more than JPEG or PNG formats and are cheaper and time effective than videos. It was because of GIFs that caused Instagram to create Boomerang.

8. The Right Hashtag Matters

Your choice of hashtag for your Instagram post can make the difference between top or bottom of the post. Use a generic hashtag and you will find yourself facing stiff competition from millions of other companies. Your best bet is to combine trending and industry-specific hashtags to find the best hashtag that will connect you to your target market.

The number of hashtags will also be critical in your marketing campaign. Instagram has a limit of of 30 hashtags but putting all of them below your caption will make it look untargeted and unprofessional. 91% of posts from top brands are limited to less than seven hashtags to get many likes. To determine the right number of hashtag for your campaign, check the number of hashtags your competitors and influencers usually use and then experiment with the number until you get it right.

9. Use Instagram traffic to boost your website traffic

By adding a clickable link in your profile, you can use Instagram traffic to boost your own traffic. Create special offers and promotions to encourage followers to click through. In addition, you should combine strong calls to action with your URL in a text overlay on any images or videos.

10. Use SEO To 'Win' Instagram

To make your business competitive, you might want to create an SEO strategy for your Instagram account. Your account handle and account name will impact your SEO. The @ name in your account will reflect the industry where your business operates. The important thing is to make sure that the content of your posts fits your handle or else they will not appear in the Explore section.

Chapter Six

YOUTUBE MARKETING 2019

Did you know that your audience loves visual content the most? Amongst visual content, videos are a favorite of the audience. Whether you own a retail business or offer B2B services, there's enormous scope with videos, to create content that would engage your audience. A lot can be done to market your brand on this video sharing platform. If you don't have a YouTube channel for your brand, you need to get one now. The best part about YouTube is that you can use your brand channel to log into multiple google accounts simultaneously. So, a YouTube channel will allow for streamlined workflow in teams.

Also, YouTube has a huge viewership. Leverage it the right way to reach out to big audience segments.

A good YouTube marketing strategy accounts for leveraging the new as well as the old.

Build Your YouTube Brand Channel

Your YouTube channel should spin out your brand's story to the people. From your channel icon to channel description, everything should speak your brand's voice. Add your brand's logo to the YouTube channel icon. Add a custom YouTube banner as well, with social media icons leading your audience to your social media handle across platforms. In the 'About' section of your YouTube channel, add a brief description of your brand. Your description should introduce every new visitor to your brand and reflect your brand voice. Put calls to action leading to your website or any other pages you want to lead your audience to.

Finally, divide your videos into different playlists. You can create branded playlists with names unique to your brand. Categorize playlists into webinars, behind the scenes etc., depending upon your video content.

2. Consistently Create And Add Compelling Videos To Your Channel

Create video content that gets your audience talking. Most importantly, use YouTube videos to bring out your brand's story.

Are you a B2B brand? You can create YouTube videos that complement your blog or website content. Bring your customers to give quick reviews of your brand. Ask them to share the experience of using your products, working with your brand and so on to take your YouTube marketing plan to the next level. Create and run a separate Video blog channel for your brand and interact with your audience using the platform regularly.

Interview industry professionals, seniors and subject matter experts. Informative video content is most popular with the audiences. Post step by step videos and tutorials on how to use your products or services. At the same time, keep posting videos consistently on your channel. Find out the right time to post content, when the audience is most active on the platform. Add videos to your channel accordingly.

3. Leverage YouTube Tools And Features

YouTube has a host of tools and features that can help you enhance your YouTube marketing strategy 2019. Use end screens and cards to add your desired calls to action. Shared a video on how to assemble a product? Lead your audience to other videos on how to use the product and other similar content from your playlists. Add transcripts your videos. Make your video content universal by adding closed captions. It cuts out the language barrier and makes your content consumable by audiences across borders. At the same time, you can reach out to the disabled with this YouTube video feature. A keyword-optimized video transcript helps enhance your YouTube SEO as well.

These incredible tools come as a part of your YouTube channel. Make the most of these, to level up on your YouTube Marketing strategy.

4. Optimize Your YouTube Video Description And Thumbnails

Since your YouTube video thumbnails and description are the ones that provide a glimpse into your content, optimize these for better results. Your YouTube thumbnail should push YouTube users to click and watch your video. The most important elements of a good YouTube thumbnail image include a picture and a caption. Add a popping image and caption that draws the attention of your audience. Use facial-close-ups for best response. The idea is to create a visual representation of the video content in the thumbnail.

Equally important in your YouTube marketing strategy 2019 is your video description. Make all your YouTube video descriptions keyword optimized to enhance YouTube SEO. Also, make sure that your YouTube video descriptions align and complement your YouTube video content. Apart from using keywords, use catchy phrases that push the users to hit the play button on your videos.

5. Add YouTube Stories To Your YouTube Marketing Strategy 2019

After Instagram and Facebook, YouTube hops on to the stories' bandwagon. YouTube now has the stories feature which allows for you to add short, mobile-only videos that expire after 7 days. YouTube offers this feature to creators with more than 10,000 subscribers on the platform. Easily create YouTube stories in a matter of seconds with the tap button on your profile and then edit them. Trim your YouTube stories and add filters, music, text, stickers, and even links to your videos. As a creator, this tool allows you to diversify on your content on the platform. With this new feature and the tools that come along with it, you can build a strong relationship with your community. It will also help you boost engagement.

Create compelling stories that generate interactions with viewers. Respond to all the comments and expand your community.

6. Optimize Video Titles For YouTube Voice Search

Enhance your YouTube SEO by optimizing title for YouTube voice search. People use YouTube voice search to find videos quickly, without having to use their fingers to type out the video titles. Since voice search is an easier, hassle free way to get YouTube video results, you need to ensure your videos appear before your audience.

Most importantly, optimize your YouTube video title to make it SEO friendly. Imagine yourself using YouTube voice search for your videos. Would you go for a longer YouTube video title or a shorter one? Most people will use a small number of keywords to describe their YouTube query.

The language will be less formal and more conversational.

So, frame a YouTube title that includes important keywords, is short and simple and has a conversational tone. This will improve your YouTube SEO to a great extent and eventually increase your views on the platform.

7. Influencer Marketing On YouTube

Include Influencer marketing as a part of your YouTube marketing strategy 2019. There are 3 main benefits of partnering with an Influencer:

• Access to a larger audience
• Access to another creator's skills
• Diversification of your content

And all these benefits add up to bring more engagement for your brand. Find out niche Influencer. Someone whose niche aligns with your brand. Using Unbox Social's social media analytics tool, track different Influencers from your niche. The Industry feed feature on the tool dashboard allows you to track as many Influencers as you want and get regular updates about them.

Monitor their activity and zero down on one Influencer. Approach them and bring them on board. You can use Influencers to churn out great quality video content. Leverage their content creation skills and influence to your best. Ask them to do product reviews, feature on your channel for account takeovers, or make them your brand ambassadors. There are many ways in which you can use Influencer marketing as a part of your YouTube marketing strategy.

At the same time keep track of all the trends and watch out for outdated Influencer marketing practices that you may be indulging in.

8. USE YOUTUBE ADS

Paid content will continue to be an integral part of a good YouTube strategy 2019. A sure shot way to make your videos appear before your audience is through the advertising option.

YouTube Ads come in 6 different formats- skippable True View in-stream Ads, 6 second bumper Ads, sponsored cards, overlay Ads, display Ads and True view Discovery Ads which appear on the homepage, alongside search results and next to related videos.

If you aren't using YouTube Ads to market your brand, do it now and check out the results for yourself.

9. Monitor Your Competitors

Monitoring your competitors is an integral part of every business and marketing strategy. Competitor analysis can easily be done by visiting their YouTube channel itself. Identify their videos with most views to identify content that most people resonate with. Use such content to draw inspiration for future video posts. Skim through their comments to find out any mentions of your brand. In case you spot your brand mentions, make sure to respond to each of the comments.

Also find out if any of their Ads are featuring on your videos. If that is the case, you can block these on the Google Ads manager.

10. Track And Report On Important Metrics To Learn From Them

An important part of YouTube marketing strategy 2019 is to track your performance and watch out for important metrics. Use a social media analytics and reporting tool such as Unbox Social.

11. Keep Up With Industry Trends And Updates

To be on top of your game in any industry, it is important to keep track of industry trends and updates. The social media industry is a dynamic one in itself. New features and trends in the industry as well as on the platform will inform your YouTube marketing plan.

Use Unbox Social's personalized feeds to derive information and daily updates on your industry from your chosen sources.

Get an edge over the others by always staying on top of news, trends and updates in your industry.

A good YouTube marketing strategy involves leveraging all the tools and features at your disposal and employing them to build engagement. It also involves keeping a watch on the industry as well as your competitors.

Here's a snapshot of pointers summing up on important tips for YouTube marketing strategy 2019:

• Build and enhance your YouTube channel, to reflect your brand voice

• Add compelling videos that add value to the audience and make sure to post consistently

• Leverage YouTube tools such as transcripts, end screens and cards and annotations

• Add an eye catching thumbnail image and optimize video descriptions for SEO

• Include YouTube stories as a part of your YouTube marketing strategy 2019 to build on your community and diversify your content

• Optimize YouTube video titles for YouTube voice search-Use simpler, shorter titles

• Use Influencer marketing for access to a larger audience, leverage another creator's skills and create versatile content

• Continue using YouTube Ads for a sure shot appearance before your target audience

• Keep track of your competitors

• Uncover insights about important video metrics using social media analytics' tools

• Stay on top of major industry trends and news

PAID YOUTUBE MARKETING

While YouTube may not look like it, the company has effective paid promotion options that you can use to get more attention for your videos, channel, or brand as a whole.

True View Instream ads are YouTube's way of creating "commercials" similar to the ones that you would see on live television. It's by far one of their most profitable and successful forms of online advertising.

When you take out a True View ad, you create a short video for your brand or channel that encourages viewers to learn more about your company. These ads often display at the beginning of a monetized video, and they can show in the middle of long videos as well.

However, non-monetized videos never show ads, so if you're looking to get a commercial on a certain channel, it's important to learn if that channel is monetized before you do anything.

You can also use True View in Display ads that show as a thumbnail next to the video someone's currently watching. These look a lot like PPC ads with a thumbnail next to them.

People click on your ads whenever they want, and they're great for promoting videos you've already made. In Display ads can also be an effective way of jump-starting or re-starting a viral campaign.

How You Pay

When you use True View ads, you're not billed the same as a regular AdWords ad for Google organic.

Instream ads are billed on a cost-per-view format. You're charged for a view whenever someone watches an ad for at least 30 seconds.

Keep in mind that most YouTube ads allow users to skip an ad after three seconds if they're using mobile or desktop devices. So if someone sees your brand for three seconds, skips the commercial, and later goes to your YouTube channel to learn more about you, you get a potential customer at no charge!

InDisplay ads are changed on a cost-per-view format as well. You're charged whenever someone clicks on your video's thumbnail and starts watching the video on a watch page.

With these two primary advertising methods, YouTube makes it incredibly easy and affordable for you to get the word out about your company and its videos.

HOW TO SET UP A PAID YOUTUBE VIDEO MARKETING AD

Unfortunately, no one has yet invented a robot that sets up YouTube video marketing ads for you. The process may sound somewhat complicated at first because the YouTube ad system is powerful, but it's fairly easy to start your first campaign. To set up a new YouTube ad, follow these steps:

• Log in to your YouTube channel by using the Sign In link.

• Go to YouTube Ads and click the Get Started with AdWords for Video button.

• Select your time zone and your preferred currency, and then click the Continue button.

• Enter a name for your campaign in the Campaign Name field.

• On the confirmation page that appears, click the Sign In to Your AdWords Account link.

• Enter the username and password for your YouTube account again.

• Now you're entering the AdWords for Video system, where you can set up your campaign.

• Enter the amount of your daily budget in the Budget field.

• It's the amount you're willing to spend per day on your ads. You can increase or decrease the budget at any time. Start with a small amount, such as $50, and increase it gradually as you start seeing the results you want.

• Click the Select Video button.

• Enter the name of your YouTube channel.

• YouTube shows you a list of your videos.

• Select the video that you want to use as an ad.

• Your YouTube ad may be the first thing that people see about your company, so use a video that's short, catchy, and to the point.

• Write your ad text.

This short bit of text appears next to the video thumbnail in your ads. You can write one headline with a maximum length of 25 characters, and you can write two lines of description text with 35 characters apiece.

• Attach a catchy title, and tell people why they should watch this video.

• Choose the thumbnail you want to use.

• Enter your website address in the Display URL field.

• If you want to direct viewers to a particular page other than your website's home page, enter a web address in the Destination URL field.

• Click the Save and Continue button to create your ad.

• Now you need to tell YouTube where to show your ad. This target selection is a targeting group.

• Create a new targeting group by first giving the target group a name in the Name field.

• Choose a maximum cost per view (CPV) amount.

This amount is the maximum you're willing to pay every time a viewer watches your video. A good amount to start with is 80 cents. You can optimize the amount later.

For in-search and in-display ads, you pay only if people click a Promoted Video ad, not for the ad simply showing up. In the case of in-stream ads, you're charged only when the viewer watches at least 30 seconds of your video ad. For in-slate ads, you pay only when someone actively chooses to view your ad. This pay per view method makes YouTube ads highly cost-effective.

• Enter three or four of the most important keywords in the Search for Targeting Suggestions field, and click the Get Targeting Suggestions button.

• Click the Expand link next to each suggestion and click the Add button next to each keyword or placement you want to add.

• If you want to refine your targets further, click the Add YouTube Search Keywords and Add Targets button in the sidebar on the right to add additional keywords and placements.

• Click the Save and Enable Targeting button to start your campaign.

• If this is the first time you buy ads on Google or YouTube, you're asked for your billing information.

YOUTUBE MARKETING TIPS 2019

Traditional marketing is slowly becoming obsolete. Brands need to prioritize digital marketing strategies to stay relevant and successful in 2019. To approach this properly, you'll need to start producing more video content.

When it comes to video, YouTube is king. The platform has more than 1.9 billion monthly active users, and 180 million hours of video content is consumed there every day.

Furthermore, 48% of people named YouTube as their favorite online video provider.

It's ranked first over Netflix, Facebook, and Hulu, which got 29%, 10%, and 7% of votes, respectively. YouTube isn't just the favorite; it's more popular than the other three networks combined.

If you think that's impressive, wait until you hear this: YouTube is the number two ranked website in the world, second only to Google, according to Alexa rankings.

The reason why YouTube is great for marketers is because its content is easy to repurpose across multiple platforms. Once you add a video to your YouTube channel, it's easy to share it on other social media sites, send it to your email subscribers, and add it to your website.

I've identified the top ten tips to enhance your YouTube videos in 2019. Use this list as a reference to help you produce better content.

1. Share links that start playback at a specific time

Once videos are uploaded to YouTube, you can share them on other platforms. But there are instances when you'll want to share only a portion of your video.

For example, maybe you're discussing a specific topic in a social media post. You realize that you've already covered this in a YouTube video.

However, the video is five minutes long. The content that's relevant to your post doesn't get addressed until the three-minute mark.

No problem. Just click on the share link to get started. (This is how you would normally share any video on YouTube.) By default, the video will play from the beginning, as expected. You have the option to change this by using the options that pop up after you click on the share button. Here's what it looks like:

YouTube start at timestamp

At the bottom of this menu, check the "Start at" box, and type the time mark at which you want the video to start playing. (Alternatively, you can pause the video before you click on the share button. The timer will automatically be set at that point. You still need to check the box for it to work.)

Once this feature is enabled, the URL's share link changes. As you can see, the link in the image above ends with "t=158." This link will start playing the video 158 seconds in, which is the 2:38 mark.

2. Add a transcript

Adding a transcript will make it easier for users to find your videos and your channel through YouTube as well as Google searches. By default, YouTube will automatically generate a transcript for all your videos once they are uploaded. You just need to make sure you haven't hidden this option from your audience. (You have the ability to edit your transcripts as well, so review them to catch any errors.)

YouTube also provides a feature for you to manually type your own transcripts as you play the video. Here's an example of what a final transcript looks like once a video is uploaded:

YouTube Transcript

In some instances, you may want a video or audio file transcribed for other purposes. For example, maybe you have a recording of a seminar you recently spoke at or of an important conference call. Now, you want to refer to the video to help you write a blog post. It's much easier to use a transcript instead of constantly having to pause, fast forward, and rewind a video to catch your speech.

Upload that content to YouTube, and get a free transcript of it. You don't have to share or publish the video on your channel if you want to keep it private. You'll still be able to get the content transcribed free.

3. Create A GIF With Any YouTube URL

GIFs are one of the top visual elements you can use to improve your marketing strategy.

Rather than using GIFs from a library everyone has access to, you can create a GIF from a YouTube video. You have the option to use either your own videos or videos from other channels.

This is very easy to do.

First, find the YouTube video with the clip you want to use. Next, insert the word "gif" after the www. The URL will go from www.youtube.com/watch to www.gifyoutube.com/watch. After you change the URL, you'll automatically get redirected to gifs.com.

The video will be ready to edit and turn into a GIF.

You've got lots of options here to make your GIF unique. Start by determining what portion of the video you want to turn into a GIF. Next, you can determine the length of your GIF. Add captions. Crop the video. Play around with effects.

Once you create your GIF, download it, and share it on your other marketing channels.

4. Organize Your Videos With Playlists

If you have lots of videos uploaded to your YouTube channel, playlists are the best way to keep them organized. When a user navigates to your channel, they will have the option to watch different playlists that have similar videos grouped together.

It will be much easier for viewers to find what they're looking for here.

YouTube also allows you to collaborate on your playlists with a friend. From your playlist settings, navigate to the "Collaborate" tab.

Once you add a collaborator, this user will be able to add videos to the playlist. This can be a useful way to manage your relationships with social influencers—simply have an influencer upload content directly to your channel through a playlist.

5. Create a custom URL

You want to make sure your business has a custom URL on YouTube. You won't get this by default.

If you have a new YouTube channel, you won't be able to create a custom URL right away. These are the requirements:

• account is 30 days old

• photo set as channel icon

• channel art uploaded

• at least 100 subscribers

Once you hit these marks, you'll be eligible to get a custom URL.

You can find this option within your account settings. Just navigate to the Advanced menu:

Before you claim your custom URL, make sure you think it through clearly: you won't have the option to change it once it gets approved.

6. Add An Actionable End Screen

What do you want a viewer to do when they finish watching one of your videos? If you want the user to keep watching more videos or visit your website, you can add these CTAs to an end screen.

From your video manager page, click the "Edit" button for the video you want to change. Then find the "End screen & Annotations" link from the drop-down menu:

A pop up will appear. Depending on your marketing goals, you can add one or more of these elements to your end page:

7. Use Enhancements To Edit Videos

You might already be using some third-party software to edit videos before you upload them to your channel. (Editing is a great way to create killer video promotions to increase engagement.) But if you don't need to do anything elaborate, you can take advantage of the YouTube enhancements feature. This allows you to edit directly on the platform.

The enhancements feature lets you add or change music and audio, apply filters, trim sections out of your video, and blur portions of it.

You can even edit content after a video has already been uploaded to your channel. However, unless you are part of the YouTube partner program, you might not be able to make all the changes to videos with more than 100,000 views.

You'll always have the option to blur faces, even if your video has more than 100,000 views and you're not part of the partner program. YouTube allows this to help protect the identity of people in your video.

8. Broadcast Live Streams

Has your business jumped on the live video bandwagon?

If not, it's time for you to hop on board. That's because 82% of people say they prefer live videos over social media posts from business profiles. Furthermore, 80% of people say they would rather watch live video content than read blog posts about a topic.

Believe it or not, consumers actually prefer YouTube live streams over Facebook Live.

YouTube allows you to go live from your desktop computer or mobile device. You can keep an archive of your live streams that were added to your YouTube channel so people can watch the content even after the stream is over. But you can disable this feature if you want.

Want to grow your audience even more? Consider this: 87% of people said they would watch more live videos if they contained behind the scenes content.

8. Upload 360-Degree Videos

We now know that 360-degree videos increase engagement rates. These videos have a 14% higher ROI than regular videos.

They also have a 46% higher completion rate than traditional videos.

This is the type of content people want to see with 360-degree videos.

When it comes to a 360-degree video, 98% of consumers living in the United States say they think it is more exciting than any other type of video.

And 90% of people believe content will be improved if it can be viewed as a 360-degree video instead of a traditional format.

Having a 360-degree video increases the chances that viewers will interact with it by 66%.

What's even more impressive is that 70% of marketers believe that adding 360-degree video content has helped improve their businesses.

9. Use Google Trends To Find Popular Search Terms

How do you know what type of content you should upload to YouTube? Try searching for keywords related to your company on Google Trends. This will show you the popularity of a search term over time and tell you whether you should be creating content on that subject.

10. Run Ads On Youtube

YouTube is owned by Google. This means you can set up YouTube ads through your Google Ads account.

You'll have the option to do the following:

- select your audience
- choose locations you want to target
- set your budget

This is very easy to do, especially if you're already using Google Ads for other purposes.

Chapter Seven

TWITTER MARKETING 2019

The world of marketing is a very dynamic field where marketers constantly fight for a bigger "piece of the pie. "It's no surprise that as the usage of social media in every aspect of our lives grows; marketing through those platforms is becoming more important and influential.

New marketing tools and techniques are persistently emerging, and according to research, content marketing is estimated to be a $400 billion industry by 2021.

When it comes to marketing on Twitter, the past year was not the best time for the social platform. Especially 2016 and 2017 when the platform was used to spread bad press about the elections happening in 2016. Abuse and bullying were present a lot on the social media platform.

Twitter, however, did react fast and implemented many changes that improved the situation of the social platform. They addressed the bullying problem and fake news, which is a very good situation for Twitter.

Twitter has always been an extremely valuable marketing tool for all types of businesses and brands. It is a highly-efficient marketing tool in itself when exercised appropriately. Quite different from how other social media channels work for your marketing strategies, working with Twitter in terms of your brand's marketing means that you get a hold of the trends in real time as your feed gets constantly updated.

FYI, 326 million people use Twitter every month. That's nine million fewer than in mid-2018, and four million fewer than late 2017. With such a huge and smart audience right out there, Twitter really lets you reach out to your target audience and gives your business a lot of desired results.

Twitter has managed to establish itself as an authoritative and authenticated brand marketing platform.

As Twitter Content marketing continues to grow and get more complex with each passing day, having a unique approach to your Twitter marketing strategy in 2019 will help you shape the way you market your content and the way your audience intends to consume it.

This makes the platform still important and a valuable marketing tool for every brand out there. There are some marketing strategies that can be specifically used on Twitter to promote a product and interact with the customers.

Tips to help:

1. Use Humor In Your Tweets

Brands that use humor in their tweets are retweeted and followed by a lot more people than others. This is the case because using humor as the voice of a brand makes people excited to re-visit the Twitter page and to share the news with their friends.

Examples of brands that practice this strategy are:

• The fast food chain Wendy's; they are using sarcastic comments while replying to their customers that is responsible for a lot of retweets.

• The mega-popular streaming service Netflix; they are using clips from their original series and making inside jokes.

• Spirit Airlines frequently makes light jokes on their Twitter account and put a positive turn on stressful situations.

2. Keep Up The Creativity And Visuals

Try to be as creative as you can, while at the same time giving personal replies as much as you can to your customers.

Getting innovative with the content of your tweets and the visuals can really impact the feedback. Keeping the same format on all tweets might get too boring. Using visuals in your tweets makes people three times more likely to engage.

3. Keep It Personalized

Customers want personalized responses when it comes to Twitter. People want to be acknowledged and are satisfied when they know that the company is listening to them.

Although there will always be a portion of customers that are just fishing for refunds, the majority of the loyal customers have valid complaints. What these people need is a sign from the company that somebody is listening and working on the issues in question. Twitter gives the opportunity for a personalized response to the customers. This way, you can also resolve issues much quicker which is why this is the preferred channel of communicating with the customer base for many important brands.

One example of a great personalized response that draws a lot of attention was the following story about Morton's Steakhouse and Peter Shankman.

Peter tweeted to Morton's Steakhouse that he would like somebody from the restaurant to meet him at the Newark Airport when his plane lands with a porterhouse steak.

He did it jokingly, but to his surprise, a server form the steakhouse met him at the airport with the steak! The story blew up on Twitter and outside of the social platform which meant a lot of good press related to Morton's Steakhouse.

4. Use hashtags property

We all know how hashtags are effective in making a fuss about a certain topic or happening. Hashtags are often used in a wrong way which makes this strategy fail.

If you're planning to include hashtags in your business's Twitter strategy, be sure that you do it the proper way. You should only hashtag keywords or short phrases in order to put the accent on something important.

If a customer clicks on a hashtag, they will be able to see other Tweets that include the hash tagged word. They can be included anywhere in a tweet, and if you're creative and your hashtag light up the Twitter community, it will be seen in Trending Topics.

PAID TWITTER MARKETING

Twitter is undeniably an important service in the business world. The microblogging website provides you with an easy-to-use platform through which you can promote your products, services, accomplishments and share news with your customers. Additionally, the social media network is a perfect way to generate leads and continue to retain their attention throughout the business-to-consumer relationship.

Recently, Twitter has grown to over 500 million users, and the service is expected to generate ad revenues upwards of $259.9 million before 2012 is finished, eMarketer reports. Therefore, you need to figure out how Twitter fits into your business model, and if you want to use paid promotional tactics or rely on quality content and share ability. While a balanced approach will often produce the most desirable results, you first need to understand the paid promotional options that Twitter has begun offering its clients.

1.) Promoted account – This option is featured in organic Twitter search results and within the Who To Follow section of the website. Promoted accounts are suggested profiles based on the followers a user already engages with through the social service.

2.) Promoted Tweets – These options appear in the timelines of users. Promoted Tweets often integrate well into non-paid Tweets, and professionals who use this marketing approach may find users engage with their content more regularly.

3.) Promoted trends – Twitter.com and the company's mobile application show trending topics based on specific time intervals. Professionals can promote a trend, and the topic will be featured in the section, so users can keep abreast of the latest posts associated with the topic. This option is an easy way to get people to talk about your company, project or service.

HOW TO ADVERTISE ON TWITTER

Choose Between "Promote Mode" And "Twitter Ads."

Promoted Tweets Vs. Twitter Ads

Promoted tweets will allow your tweets to appear in the Twitter streams or Twitter search results of specific users. Running Twitter Ads is a more holistic campaign, using multiple groups of tweets to accomplish a single goal for your brand. Depending on your objective, Twitter Ads can display your username in places other than a user's newsfeed, such as the "Who to Follow" section to the right of their Twitter homepage.

How Do I Choose?

If you're simply looking to get more eyeballs on a webpage, promoted tweets might be just the thing you need. In this option, you pay a flat monthly fee for as long as you're promoting a tweet. It's perfect for gaining focused exposure on (and generating leads from) a particular aspect of your business.

If you're looking to grow your follower base and/or build up your audience, Twitter Ads offer a bit more firepower. In the steps below, you'll learn how to harness it.

2. Select Your Twitter Ad's Objective.

Promoted tweets are fairly easy to set up, and you can learn about this process in the section at the bottom of this blog post. To launch a Twitter Ad campaign, however, your next step is determining your objective

- App installs

- Followers

- Tweet engagements

- Promoted video views

- Website clicks or conversions

- App re-engagements

- In-stream video views (pre-roll)

- Awareness

Promoted Accounts

Ad campaigns focused on followers, the second objective listed above, are also known as "Promoted Accounts." This type of campaign allows you to promote your profile, rather than a series of tweets, in your target audience's newsfeeds and on the profile pages of the other accounts they care about.

3. Fill In The Details Your Ad Campaign.

Once you choose an objective, you'll be taken to a page where you can name your campaign, a start and end date for your campaign, and your campaign's total budget. Depending on the objective you chose in Step 2, you might have other details to fill in that are unique to your ad.

When determining how much money you want to invest in a Twitter Ads campaign, you'll set a daily budget and an optional total budget. Throughout the day, your daily budget will pay

Twitter your set amount at the specific cadence you can set yourself.

The cadence of your promoted content can be set to "Standard (recommended)," which shows ads to your target audience at intervals Twitter deems most efficient; or "Accelerated," which shows your ads as much as possible throughout the day. Accelerated ads cater to ad campaigns you want to perform well in a short amount of time.

4. Create an ad group within your campaign.

Next, you'll create an ad group for your campaign -- there should be at least one pre-created on the left-hand side of your Twitter Ads page. To create more than one ad group, select "Copy ad group" to the right-hand side of your current ad group and you'll see new ones appear in your ad campaign's framework, as shown above.

Ad groups are individual ads that consist of their own budgets, audiences, and start and end times but operate under the umbrella of your larger campaign.

For example, if you have a two-week Twitter Ads campaign with the objective of website clicks and a budget of $100, you can also create one or more ad groups that run for just a couple of days each, promote separate webpages on your website, and target different types of Twitter users. You'll see how to set these parameters in the next few steps.

In the "Details" tab, shown above, enter an ad group name, a start and end time, a budget for the ad group, and a bid type. Bid types allow you to "bid" on a promoted ad placement. Ad placements will cost different amounts depending on your audience and where the ad appears on Twitter, and you can set your ad group to bid for placement in one of three ways:

• Automatic bid: This type of bid permits Twitter to bill you the most cost-effective amount every time your audience engages with your ad content. The cost Twitter bills you is based on your ad group's budget and audience parameters.

• Maximum bid: This type of bid gives you full control over how much money you're willing to pay every time your audience engages with your ad content.

• Target bid: This type of bid allows you to specify how much money from your ad group's budget you'd like Twitter to bill you every time your audience engages with your ad content. The price you're billed will reflect the daily average cost of each ad placement within your audience.

5. Select Your Target Audience For Each Ad Group.

Beneath the "Details" tab of your ad group, select "Targeting." This is where you'll set the parameters of your target audience.

It's important to customize your audience to be a good fit for your company and your message. That way, you're only paying for engagement from folks who might have some interest in downloading your content or learning more about your product or service. A more targeted audience is more likely to help you generate qualified leads.

What Are My Options?

To select an audience for each ad group you create, you'll customize the following criteria:

• Gender: If your product or service caters primarily to either males or females, you should take advantage of the gender targeting option.

• Age: Setting an age range is helpful for advertisements that are promoting a product or event that has either a particular age restriction or scope of interest.

• Location: You'll want to target by location if you run a local business, or if you sell primarily to specific regions (whether that's your city or North America).

• Language: This criterion might need to be used in tandem with the location filter, described above, if an ad is targeting a region of the world that speaks a language other than English.

• Device: This is a great targeting option if your product or service caters more specifically to people on the go, or if your website visitors are most likely to convert on your offer when they're in the office.

• Audience features: These include keywords, movies & shows, conversation topics, events, and related interests.

You can also select which devices you'd like your promoted tweets to be displayed on -- any combination of desktop and the various mobile devices.

Targeting By Keywords

Targeting by "keywords" -- an option included in the "Audience features" field, listed above -- allows you to reach people that search, tweet about, or engage with specific keywords. For example, if I'm promoting Hub Spot's eBooks, How to Use Twitter for Business, I might filter my audience by keywords I consider relevant to this advertisement, like this:

This audience targeting criterion is helpful if you want to know exactly how many Twitter users are currently using a keyword. As you can see in the screenshot above, the keyword "marketing" is being used by 7.67 million people. This data can help you decide between topics that seem similar but have different levels of popularity you wouldn't know about otherwise.

Targeting By Interests And Followers

Targeting by interests and followers allows you to create a list of Twitter usernames and then target users whose interests are similar to the interests of those users' followers.

A great use of this type of targeting is when compiling a small list of the top influencers in your industry. For example, to promote HubSpot's how to Use Twitter for Business eBooks, I'll want to target an audience of users interested in social media. Targeting by interests and followers allows me to say, "show these tweets to people who are like so-and-so's followers." As a result, I've created a large audience that's still tailored to the topic of my content.

With this targeting option, you can also add a list of interest categories. So, for example, I could say, "show these tweets to people interested in marketing, social media, or lead generation." Again, this creates a broad audience focused on the topic of the content or products you're promoting.

6. Select The Creatives You'd Like To Run With Each Ad Group.

Your last task in creating a Twitter Ads campaign is to choose the creatives you want to run with each ad group belonging to your campaign. "Creatives" are simply the tweets you want to promote, and you can select them from the list of tweets that appear under each ad group's Creatives tab. Select the "Creatives" tab beneath the Targeting tab to get started.

This is the fun part. You can either select from existing tweets in your account or create new ones.

To compose a new tweet, click the blue quill icon to the far right of your Creatives screen. When crafting a new tweet, you can check the "Promoted-only" button if you'd only like to promote it through your Twitter Ads campaign, and not have the tweet appear organically on your followers' newsfeeds. See what this option looks like below.

In addition to promoting your tweets on your audiences' timelines, you can also choose to have your tweets appear in users' profiles and the detail pages of specific twitter conversations. The benefit of this type of targeting is that it helps you define a more qualified audience, since these people are actively looking for or engaging with those specific keywords that are relevant to your offer. You can select this option on the right-hand side of your Creatives tab

7. Review And Launch Your Campaign.

Finally, select the "Review your campaign" button, as shown above, to look over your campaign details. If everything looks correct, hit "Launch campaign" at the top-right-hand corner of your screen to run the campaign.

How To Promote A Tweet

Promoting tweets allows you to show critical pieces of content to a wide audience and drive views to the landing pages that generate leads for your business. This Twitter Ads option gives you a lot more flexibility in terms of the content you want potential viewers and customers to see.

Here's a quick definition of this ad so you can understand how it differs from the ad campaign we walked you through in the above section:

Promoted tweets are paid advertisements that Twitter places in front of your target audience based on their interests or location. Each ad supports a single tweet, and you can customize the audience of each individual ad. Currently, businesses can only promote tweets in the U.S., U.K., and Japan.

Here's how to promote a tweet:

1. Select "Promote Mode" from the campaign menu and click "Get started."

You'll start from the same place you start when creating a full, multi-tweet Twitter Ads campaign: This menu screen. Once there, click "Get started." When you're done, click "Next" on the top-right-hand corner of the page.

2. Select Your Promoted Tweet's Country And Time zone.

Currently, you can only promote tweets to audiences in the U.S., the U.K., and Japan. Start creating your ad by selecting of these three options, as well as your intended time zone. When you're done, click "Next" on the top-right-hand corner of the page.

3. Choose Either "Interests" Or "Location" As Your Targeting Method.

Twitter can promote tweets to an audience based on their interests or location. Choose one of these methods and follow Step 4 or Step 5, below, depending on your choice.

4. Choose Up To Five Interests Associated With Your Target Audience.

If you choose to target an audience based on their interests, select this option, hit "Next," and Twitter will take you to the page shown above. Here, you can select a maximum of five interests related to your ideal audience.

Keep in mind the more interests you select, the more types of people your promoted tweet will appear in front of.

5. Choose Up To Five Locations Associated With Your Target Audience.

If you choose to target an audience based on their location, select this option, hit "Next," and Twitter will take you to the page shown above. Here, you can search a specific city, state, and country where you want your ad to appear.

You can select up to five locations where you'd like your tweet to be promoted. Keep in mind you can only place promoted tweets in front of users who live in the U.S., the U.K., or Japan.

6. Review Your Ad Criteria And Select "Proceed."

Once you've customized your audience's interests or location, hit "Next" and Twitter will show you an overview of your ad criteria, including your bill.

The cost to promote a tweet has changed since Twitter first began offering this type of ad. Unlike Twitter Ads campaigns, promoted tweets currently cost a flat monthly fee of $99 per month. Each new tweet you promote will carry a separate monthly fee.

Sound good to you? Review your ad criteria and check that you agree to the Twitter Promote Mode's Terms of Service at the bottom of this page. Then, click "Proceed" on the top-right-hand corner of your screen.

7. Add Your Billing Information And Launch Your Promoted Tweet.

If you haven't yet added billing information, Twitter will ask you to enter it in the following screen. Select "Save" and follow the prompts to officially promote your tweet.

There you have it! No matter which type of Twitter ad you create, be sure to keep an eye on your campaigns as they run and continue to optimize them for better results in the future.

TWITTER MARKETING TIPS 2019

As the Social Media Manager for @TwitterBusiness, it's my job to learn and share tips that help brands make the most of Twitter. Helping me in this is the fact that not too long ago I was one of these brands. I was a Social Media Manager, and before that an Agency Account Manager, trying to navigate the platform and understand its place in my planning. I know firsthand that Twitter can be a little intimidating, and firsthand that it doesn't have to be.

In that spirit, here are five things I've learned working at Twitter that I wish I'd known sooner, and my hopes that they can help inform your 2019 planning.

Twitter Is What's Happening

Did you know that Twitter is listed as a news app in the apple app store — not as a social media app? If you use Twitter, this probably isn't so surprising.

Twitter is a place where you can connect beyond just your friends and family, to a global network to know what's happening, right now. A stranger across the globe can be your real-time eye-witness to tomorrow's headline.

2019 advice: Break your news here. This might be something major, like a product launch, or smaller, like a picture of your new office plant. Use Twitter to share what's new in your company's world so your followers feel like they're right there with you.

"Look At Me" Vs "Look At This"

Twitter is a place where people use the front — and back — facing camera. You will certainly find the ever-popular selfie, but the spirit of Twitter is much more focused on "look what I see" not "see what I look like." It's about sharing your point of view, literally or figuratively.

2019 advice: Vary your content to include more than promotional posts (the equivalent of selfies). Show your audience something, teach them something — turn the attention outward to connect on a more natural level.

Conversation

The magic of Twitter isn't always in the original Tweet. It's in the reply to that Tweet. And then the reply to that. It's the debate and banter that differentiates the platform.

2019 advice: Don't be afraid to Tweet text-only Tweets. It could be a question, an observation — even an open prompt asking for replies. Respond to your own replies where it makes sense. Don't want to go first? Look for existing Tweets you can reply to.

Brand voice

Twitter is the place for brands to show their personality — and it's ok if you're not sure exactly what that is. Like any personality, chances are your brand's has many sides to it, and the only way to find the best one is to experiment.

2019 advice: Don't be afraid to test a new tone, whether it be sillier, softer — whatever you're curious to explore. "Trying something" is a valid strategy. Establish guardrails (what words or topics your brand wants to avoid engaging in), experiment, and let the engagement tell you what resonates.

Events And Holidays

There are so. Many. Holidays. What you may think is a regular Tuesday might just be #NationalDonutDayor #NationalDressUpYourPetDay (it's real). These holidays become conversations, giving your brand an opportunity to engage with your audience in an organic way.

Chapter Eight

LINKEDIN MARKETING 2019

LinkedIn is an excellent platform for professionals and businesses to connect with each other; however, are the connections always meaningful? The platform is surely trying to make it so. LinkedIn has lagged behind Facebook when it comes to offering its marketers options for ad formats, targeting, and content features. With the release of "LinkedIn Pages" (replacing "Company Pages") and updated advertising tools, the New Year is a great time to get back into marketing on the web's largest professional network. For business owners and professionals looking to grow their business and build relationships, LinkedIn has got you covered.

LinkedIn remains the #1 social media platforms for professionals to connect, engage and grow their business and brand. Whether you work for a company or yourself, LinkedIn is the place to be for B2B connections, leads and sales

New LinkedIn Pages

Whether you work for a large corporation or small agency, marketing on LinkedIn has become a necessity for almost every type of business. Even business owners who are marketing to consumers can benefit from building professional relationships and sharing content of their own. LinkedIn has rebuilt their company pages to offer a multitude of new features that make connecting easier than ever

Page Layout

Before LinkedIn's Pages rollout, there were a few missing features when compared to Facebook's Business Pages. Not only can you now associate your LinkedIn Page with hashtags to join conversations about your business or industry, but there's also a

136

customizable call-to-action button just like Facebook's Business Pages. Starting a conversation with a prospective employee or customer is now achievable with the click of a button. LinkedIn wants to ensure your connections turn into real relationships--with a page built to attract and convert, they are definitely moving in the right direction.

Mobile App Updates

Sure, LinkedIn's mobile app let you post images and video to company pages before, but now admins can even share documents, PowerPoint presentations and PDFs to enhance their brand's storytelling. Facebook may have more options to display images, like in slideshows or photo galleries, but LinkedIn has one-upped them when it comes to sharing professional work. Telling engaging stories about your company on the go is seamless with LinkedIn Pages.

Content Suggestions

Ever wonder what your audience and connections actually want to see from you on their LinkedIn feeds? With Content Suggestions, businesses can see what type of content their target audience is engaged with on the platform. With recommended articles and posts, these insights can liven up a previously dull content strategy with new and trending topics. Of course, you'll want to create content of your own instead of only curating;

however, when you're busy running a business, a little help with suggestions goes a long way.

Post Sharing

Want to share a customer testimonial or product review to your company's LinkedIn Page? Now you can. Prior to LinkedIn's update, only personal profiles could share content in this way. LinkedIn has made it as easy Facebook to share conversations and posts about your business. This can really come in handy considering the number of professional groups and conversations floating around on the platform. Having a share feature makes it easy to share employee posts to Pages, making the ever beneficial employee advocacy that much simpler.

Sponsored In Mail + Sponsored Content

Mastering organic content and page optimization aren't the only LinkedIn strategies you'll want to take advantage of in 2019. Advertising on social media has become a vital part of marketing strategies for businesses of all sizes. In a recent study by Google, buyers consume an average of 10.4 pieces of content before making a purchase decision. Are you showing your audience enough valuable content to interest them enough that they want to convert? Showing one ad with a call-to-action likely won't cut it.

Combining two different methods of advertising on LinkedIn will help create a sales funnel to guide your customer along the way. Sponsored Content ("feed ads") is a great way to increase awareness of your posts, company news, events, and other content like blogs by adding a budget to them; this gives your target audience an opportunity to learn about your business or brand by seeing it in their feed, rather than directly market a product or service to them before they know who you are. Sponsored In Mail ("message ads") helps convert your audience by sending interested LinkedIn users a direct message on the app that is written and prepared by you--complete with a headline, info, and call-to-action! By joining ad format forces, you're ready to reach, connect and convert with your audience on LinkedIn.

Getting Connected

LinkedIn has a professional network of over 590 million users. It's pretty hard to deny the power of connecting with like-minded industry professionals and customers ready to start a conversation. It can become difficult or time-consuming building and maintaining a presence on any social media platform, let alone getting a return on your advertising efforts.

I have compiled the top 10 LinkedIn marketing tips for the start of 2019.

1. Update Your Profile (Even if you think it doesn't need it)

Every year it's a good habit to update your LinkedIn profile. Simply by refreshing your profile it appears differently to people – relevant! Your ideal clients, referral partner and colleagues are all looking and how you show up on your profile matters and could mean more opportunities. Here are the areas I would focus on:

• Update your professional photo – remember, first impressions matter

• Create a custom cover image for the top of your profile – think of this as a billboard for your brand

• Review your headline. We have seconds to attract someone to our profile, thus your headline must be compelling and attract those you want to connect with.

• Contact information: be sure it is updated and includes your website, email at a minimum

• Review your summary – this is where you share your career story and let people in to who you are, what makes you credible and interesting. You have 2000 character, use the space wisely.

2. Clean Up Your Network Connections

Chances are you have dozens or more connections you don't know. It worth a little effort to disconnect from people you doesn't know or haven't communicated with. This matters because LinkedIn decides (or the algorithm decides) which of your connections will be seeing your content. Why take the chance that the wrong people are seeing what you post versus people you want to influence when you post.

It's also good to get in the habit of being more intentional with developing a network and nurturing your key connections. Having more people isn't better if you never communicate with them.

3. Clean Up And Train The Newsfeed

People like to complain about posts they see in the newsfeed of their home page, but did you know you have some control over what you see? Next time you see a post that you don't want to see or from someone who is annoying because they over post go to the 3 dots in the upper of the post and from the drop-down menu choose 'Hide this post.'

The more posts you hide you can train the LinkedIn algorithm to stop showing you posts from a particular person or content posts you don't care about. Also note, from the drop-down menu

you can choose 'Unfollow' if the post is from someone you are connected to and you no longer want to see their posts in your newsfeed.

Think of this clean up as a strategy to train the system to show you post from people and organizations you actually care about and want to engage with. I hope you will invest some time in cleaning up your news feed.

4. Gain More Exposure By Posting An Update More Frequently

Every time you publish a post or article on LinkedIn the algorithm determines whether your content shows up in the feed and how far of an audience it reaches.

Posting styles below are in order of getting the highest views: (all subject to change of course)

• Text only posts: Up to 1300 characters available on a personal post

• Text & image: only add an image if it really adds to the value of your post

• Video post: keep it under a minute and only talk about one topic.

• Text with a link off the site: LinkedIn as with other social sites wants to keep you on their site as long as possible so they give less favor to outbound links.

There are 2 options for using links:

First one is best – Before the link, write context about what it is and why people might want to read it and clearly mention the link to the article is below in the comments. (You must go back and add this to the comments after you publish your post)

Second – Before the link, write context about what it is and why people might want to read it. Write this in a way that tells a story and engages with your reader. If you keep them reading the post, they'll be more likely to click through.

5. Try Native Video To Drive More Engagement

Native video is 5x more likely than other types of content to start a conversation among your connections and network. As mentioned in #3 above, video posts are fast becoming a winning way to drive engagement and having an engagement strategy will save you time and you'll see better results.

LinkedIn video pioneer & expert Goldie Chan recommends

• Get to your key takeaway immediately or you will lose your audience

• Limit each video to 1 minute and focus on one simple subject that provides value

Although your videos can be up to 10 minutes, LinkedIn viewers don't want to watch a 10-minute rambling vlog that lacks a clear point.

Additional tips for using video effectively on LinkedIn include:

• Add captions to your clip

You need to add captions to your video because people likely have the sound turned off. People will see your video in the LinkedIn feed and the video plays automatically. Most people don't want the sound to come on as they're scrolling. So, adding captions makes your video content as easy as possible to consume.

Tools: Clips App or iOS clip-o-matic App. With Clipomatic, you have to use the app's built-in camera and record the video in one shot.

With Clipomatic, you have to use the app's built-in camera and record the video in one shot.

If you are savvy, edit the first second of your video to show the image you'd like to appear as a thumbnail. Make sure you're not making a weird face!

6. Update Your Recommendations

We live in a world where social proof results in sales. Simply said, whether we want a recommendation for a restaurant or for a vendor to provide a service we're looking for, we have become trained to read a review or recommendation before making a buying decision. If you want to be considered or referred, then having a profile with up to date recommendations can give you a competitive advantage.

I suggest you gain one new recommendation per quarter. You become more relevant, and it lets people know that you are doing business and people are recommending you now – not what you did 5 years ago.

It's also a good idea when requesting a recommendation that you be specific in your request based on what you want to be known for and the results you delivered for your customer. Never send the default recommendation request because you want to be in control of the direction you want the recommendation to be written. Also, it's not enough to have a generic character recommendation, although nice – it won't necessarily get you the business. People want results.

Once posted to your LinkedIn profile, you can copy & paste the recommendations elsewhere in your marketing.

7. Consistency Versus Randomness Builds Trust & Wins Business

Showing up with consistency can win business when you are adding value each time you show up online and offline. In terms of LinkedIn how you show up is via communications with your connections via messaging, creating posts that are thoughtful and demonstrate what you stand for or have an expertise in and posting or messaging content of value. Your messages are building trust with those who are watching and believe me there are lots of lurkers out there watching who may not ever leave a comment or message you.

However, by your adding thoughtful comments to someone's post build's your trust and if you are strategic with choosing who to follow and comment on, all the better influence you will have. Being consistent on LinkedIn will keep you top of mind and so often those that show up and have built a reputation of trust and helpfulness win business.

8. Build Relationships By Helping Others

In my experience, those people who demonstrate real caring and who are authentic in helping others build mutually beneficial relationships results in more long-term opportunities. Not only that, you also position yourself as someone with knowledge, experience, resources and I think also as a leader. As a leader your team along with internal and external customers are attracted to those who demonstrate real caring to be helpful.

According to John Hall, CEO and author of Top of Mind (one of my favorite books) says "helpfulness is not a science; it's a personal, intimate practice." Below is a partial list of his best helpfulness practices.

• Share Knowledge–when you offer someone useful information, you're providing a real form of currency.

• Connect People with What They Value – This requires active listening to uncover what someone values. In business, offering unhelpful information can cost you credibility and weaken your relationships.

• Share Resources – This could be resources your company has invested in that may be idle or other resources that you know could help someone else.

• Make People Aware of Opportunities – Whenever you hear of an opportunity – whether in the form of a potential partnership, an exciting event or a journalist looking for industry contacts. Connecting the people in your network to these strategic opportunities generates trust and goodwill.

9. Leave A Voice Message Via The Linkedin Mobile App

Stand out differently with your connections by leaving a voice message inside the messenger feature – only available on the mobile app.

By recording a brief message, your contact can hear your voice and if it is brief and to the point often will respond before a basic text message. Inside the messenger on mobile in addition to the voice message, you can attach a document, picture or a stock GIF file.

10. Utilize Saved Searches & Get Leads Dropped To Your In-Box

If you have a free LinkedIn account this strategy is for you. If you have refined your ideal customer title and want to know when new people with that title fall into your criteria, simply click on 'Create a search alert' and save your search. LinkedIn then emails you any new people with your search criteria directly to your inbox. You can manage your search alerts from the same area. If

you subscribe to LinkedIn's sales navigator tool, you have the ability to save your searches within the program. I find this feature is highly unused by free account holders.

PAID LINKEDIN MARKETING

How To Get Started With Linkedin Paid Ads

There are lots of ways to spend your digital advertising budget today; but, have you considered LinkedIn? Advertising on LinkedIn is a great choice for many businesses. Below, we'll explore why you should consider it and provide a walk-through of how to create your first LinkedIn ad campaign.

Why LinkedIn Gets Overlooked

Have you run a campaign on LinkedIn? If not, you are hardly alone. LinkedIn's self-service ad platform often gets overlooked by today's marketers and media planners. This could be due to a number of misconceptions or challenges such as:

• LinkedIn is not a typical social network; but, it isn't a true content platform, either.

• LinkedIn is focused on business connections; so, marketers tend to think of it as B2B only.

• LinkedIn has a much, much smaller audience than Google or Facebook.

• LinkedIn lacks the integration of professional bid management platforms.

Understanding The Value For Marketers

Personally, I think of LinkedIn as a highly-targeted communications channel that offers marketers great opportunity. For starters, it has considerable reach — +259 million members worldwide, with an estimated 100 million in the US.

And, while some might dismiss its "smaller" audience, LinkedIn can actually help you achieve a very precise reach. This is largely due to two factors:

• LinkedIn provides great targeting options, including the ability to target by job title, employer, role, skills, and interests;

• LinkedIn profiles contain more detailed and up-to-date "professional" information compared to what people list on their personal profiles on Facebook, etc.

Beyond that, LinkedIn now provides additional value through content with its "Influencers" and "Pulse" efforts. Between both of these initiatives and the value of updates and shared stories, LinkedIn has evolved into more of a content platform that is providing a professional and exciting news feed.

In addition, LinkedIn's self-service advertising platform has a similar feel to those offered by Google and Facebook. For example, it allows you to design different types of ads, create logical groupings, define bids for specific campaigns, and measure performance with metrics such as impressions, clicks and conversions (if tagged/collected).

Is Linkedin Right For You?

Now that you know why you should consider LinkedIn for advertising, it's time to figure out if the platform would be a good fit for your needs. Whenever I look at a campaign, I ask myself a few key questions (see below). If I can answer "yes" to any of them, I know that LinkedIn ads are the right choice for the job:

1. Do I Know The Job Titles Of My Target Audience?

Since LinkedIn offers targeting by job title, it can help you pinpoint your audience. For example, if you are running the marketing department for a law school that helps legal assistants become attorneys, this targeting option would enable you to focus your efforts on the individuals who have "legal assistant" as their job title. As you can see below, there are over 100,000 of them on LinkedIn.

2. Do I Know Where My Target Audience Works?

This targeting method could be used for a number of different purposes. Organizations could tap into it for recruiting by using it to target competitors' employees. It could also be used for a targeted sales approach as it can get your brand in front of the right people at a company you are trying to sell to. In addition, this targeting option could be a great job search tool — individuals could use it to get their name in front of decisions makers at a firm they want to work for.

3. Does my target audience have unique skills/interests?

The ability to target by skills and/or interest is great for all kinds of professional businesses. For example, a vendor of analytics software could use it to target individuals who have competitive software or specific analytics languages listed in the skills section of their LinkedIn profile.

4. Do I Know The Type Of Role My Target Audience Holds At A Company, Or Their Level Of Seniority?

This might sound like a stereotype, but targeting by role can be very useful, as it allows you to gauge a person's influence level and salary.

HOW TO CREATE A LINKEDIN AD CAMPAIGN

Now that you have some ideas on how to target individuals on LinkedIn, let's do a quick walk-through on how to create an ad campaign.

Getting Started:

To create a campaign, you'll first need the following:

• A LinkedIn account

• Basic understanding of your audience

• Ad copy

• Video (optional)

Now go to the LinkedIn Ads login page and click on "Get started." This will present you with two types of campaign options: (1) Create an ad; (2) Sponsor an update.

Click on "Create an ad."

Step 1: Create Your Ad

You should now be looking at the following screen:

This is where you create your ad. To do so, you'll need to fill in a few fields:

Campaign Name: Create a name for your campaign. I recommend following any naming conventions you use on other platforms.

• Ad Language: Select the language for your ad.

• Media Type: Select either a basic advertisement that follows the traditional format, or a video ad that includes a play button on the image.

• Ad Destination: This will allow you to link your ad to either a LinkedIn profile page or an external URL. If you are driving traffic to your website, I highly recommend that you tag your URLs so that you can measure the engagement and quality of traffic in your analytics platform. If you are not familiar with the tagging of URLs, there are numerous URL tagging tools (like this one).

• Ad Design: Create your headline and description. Note that LinkedIn is a bit limited in this regard. The headline has a 25-character limit, and the description cannot exceed 75 characters (2 lines). You can also add your imagery here. Note that as you edit your ads, a thumbnail preview appears on the right side. The preview also allows you to toggle the ad size. Make sure you carefully inspect the ad preview to ensure that the image you used is visible and eye-catching.

• Ad Variations: LinkedIn allows you to create multiple variations of ads. For each ad, you can choose either an external URL or a page on LinkedIn. Note that the choice of location does not affect the price — it costs just as much to send traffic to external pages as it does to send it to internal pages. Also, keep in mind that LinkedIn advertising is push advertising, not pull. That means that your audience is not actively looking for your product or service, so you have to work harder to make sure your ad stands out and captures the user's attention. For example, I have seen q

-style headlines get better engagement than statement headlines.

Step 2: Targeting

Once you've completed your ad, it's time to focus on targeting. This is where you can really start to leverage the power of LinkedIn. While some of the targeting options on this platform are very similar to Facebook and Twitter (target by age, friends, company, etc.), LinkedIn allows you to go to the next level. As mentioned earlier, you can target people by job title, employer, industry, and even skills/ interests.

Note that as you pick options, the preview screen on the right shows you your possible reach. Be sure you understand audience size, as it is different from possible impressions or metrics used by other networks.

On LinkedIn, audience size is the number of profiles matching the criteria you have. So, while you might have 2 million registered Math Professors, they might only log in once a month vs. a marketing or IT person who logs in daily.

For example, as I define the location for our sample campaign (United States) and the skills (Tableau, Spotfire, or Data Visualization), LinkedIn tells me that I have 28,793 possible users to show my ad to.

If you feel that your audience size is getting too small, pay attention to LinkedIn's suggested options. This feature is very similar to Google's keyword recommendations. For example, when I add Tableau and Spotfire as skills, LinkedIn suggests that I might want to include the following:

When I add Google Analytics to the list of skills in my ad and then choose a non-teenage segment, I get the following audience size, which seems like a great match for my awareness goal:

Keep in mind that the more granular you go with your audience design, the better your ROI will be. For instance, I could create one campaign for Tableau and one for Spotfire, with custom ad copy for each. This approach would deliver a much higher CTR and much more targeted information.

Also, adding the LinkedIn Audience network can expand your reach (it is similar to Google's Display Network), though I'm not including it in our example.

I also wanted to mention another valuable aspect of a LinkedIn campaign — the ability to turn on "Lead Collection." This feature allows users who engaged with your ad to send you their contact info and ask to be contacted. It is very similar to a contact form approach, but due to its tight integration with the platform, it's effortless for the user and has a more secure feel to it.

Step 3: Budgeting

Last but not least, it's time to turn our attention to costs. LinkedIn offers two basic pricing models: CPC (cost-per-click) and CPM (cost per 1,000 impressions). The cost-per-click model has a minimum CPC of $2 — which definitely makes it a higher cost network than Google or Facebook. LinkedIn also offers a suggested bid range to reach the top position.

Personally, I have found that LinkedIn ads are more successful when used for narrow reach efforts. For instance, I tend to use it to reach a very specific segment. Often, I have 20 campaigns running, each with an audience of 5,000. This way, I can have a highly-targeted audience see a highly-targeted ad, and then land on a highly-targeted landing page. Using this approach, I have seen CPC deliver a much better ROI, especially since I have found that click-through rates on LinkedIn tend to be much lower than on other sites. Going by my sample campaign below, I think an average CPC of $2 would be too high, as it is purely an awareness goal. However, if I was operating Marketing Land, that price might make sense. I imagine the return visit rate and linked conference and advertising earnings would be fairly high. Therefore, acquiring a new user at a cost of $2 might be good ROI.

In terms of budget, LinkedIn has a minimum daily budget of $10. In order to successfully evaluate ad variations, I recommend having at least enough budget for 100 clicks a day. Again, LinkedIn should be about connecting with a very specific audience, so every click should be worth it.

Step 4: Submit Your Ad

The final step in the process is to submit your ad by simply clicking on "Launch Campaign." Note that LinkedIn reviews almost all ads manually, so your campaign won't be online until it goes through a quick review process

Again, when it comes to spending your digital advertising dollars, you have lots of options. Hopefully, this brief article has given you some ideas on how you might leverage LinkedIn's advertising platform for your next campaign.

Personally, I've had some good results on LinkedIn, but I'm curious if you have tried the platform.

CONCLUSION

Social media marketing is not just another way to get traffic to your blog, but it is a place where a whole lot of targeted users can be found and extracted to your site. Social media sites, as we all know are home to millions and millions of people from all over the world.

If you really want to run a successful Internet marketing campaign, it will pay you to learn a few social media marketing tips, and apply them to your efforts. Simple tips can create lasting results, and sometimes propel a company to instant success. Remember though, that instant success is the exception, not the rule, and always follow the most important tip of all: Be Patient.

The smart internet promotion expert is always looking for social media marketing tips because he knows that the competition is keen for online followers. Do not give into the temptation of using community based sites primarily to send out promotional messages because your messages will be blocked and you will lose any chance of building your client base. Create sincere online relationships with your followers before sending promotional messages.

Word of mouth is a powerful tool, and many social media marketing tips point out that your best promotion comes from allowing others to sell you to their associates. To do this, you have to provide quality content, informative information, and products that appeal to people enough that they want to talk about them to their friends. Social networking is all about communication and sharing.

In general, the more specific and strategic you can get with your social media marketing plan, the more effective you'll be in its implementation. Whether it's Twitter, Facebook, Pinterest or Instagram, there's so much you can do in the way of marketing and creating new opportunities for yourself while adding tremendous value to your clients, customers and readers. Don't make your social media marketing strategy so lofty and broad that it's unattainable. Balance is key. Always keep your customers and audience in mind. A good business objective will guide your actions, but it will also be a measure by which you determine whether you're succeeding or failing.

Do Not Go Yet; One Last Thing To Do

If you enjoyed this book or found it useful I'd be very grateful if you'd post a short review on Amazon. Your support really does make a difference and I read all the reviews personally so I can get your feedback and make this book even better.

Thanks again for your support!

CPSIA information can be obtained
at www.ICGtesting.com
Printed in the USA
BVHW040652190621
609966BV00007B/148